WORLD'S GRE

MOVIE MUSIC

Easy Piano

40 of the Most Popular and Best Loved
Movie Hits of All Time

Arranged by
DAN COATES

This collection includes 40 of the most popular pieces of music ever written for the movies. Some of the music became popular independently of the film; others will always be associated with a particular motion picture. Music is an essential component of almost every movie. It can heighten the emotion of a scene, further the action, or foreshadow things to come. Who can forget a young Dorothy imagining a life outside of Kansas ("Over the Rainbow"), or Rocky Balboa victoriously running up the steps of the Philadelphia Museum of Art ("Gonna Fly Now"), or Kermit the Frog gently singing about dreamers ("The Rainbow Connection")? All of these moments are permanently etched into our memories, thanks to the extraordinary combination of music and action.

World's Greatest Movie Music embraces many styles of music that are included in motion pictures. From triumphant orchestral themes ("Star Wars" and "Raiders March") to songs that found a life on the pop charts ("Stayin' Alive," "I Don't Want to Miss a Thing," and "Raindrops Keep Fallin' on My Head"), there is something very special for everyone in this collection.

Each selection is arranged by Dan Coates, a master of creating full sounding music that can be read almost at sight. So, dim the lights, turn the page, and enjoy performing some of the greatest film music ever written.

Copyright © MMIX by Alfred Music
All rights reserved
ISBN-10: 0-7390-6177-1
ISBN-13: 978-0-7390-6177-0

CONTENTS

Title	Movie	Page
And All That Jazz	Chicago	4
Arthur's Theme (Best That You Can Do)	Arthur	10
As Time Goes By	Casablanca	26
Be Our Guest	Beauty and the Beast	14
Beauty and the Beast	Beauty and the Beast	18
Believe	The Polar Express	22
Can You Feel the Love Tonight	The Lion King	29
Colors of the Wind	Pocahontas	34
The Days of Wine and Roses	The Days of Wine and Roses	32
Endless Love	Endless Love	39
Evergreen	A Star Is Born	44
Eye of the Tiger	Rocky III	48
Fame	Fame	54
Georgy Girl	Georgy Girl	51
Gonna Fly Now	Rocky	58
Hedwig's Theme	Harry Potter	62
I Don't Want to Miss a Thing	Armageddon	66
In Dreams	The Lord of the Rings: The Fellowship of the Ring	70
James Bond Theme	James Bond	73
Laura	Laura	76

Title	Movie	Page
Love Is a Many Splendored Thing	*Love Is a Many Splendored Thing* . .	79
Old Time Rock and Roll	*Risky Business*	82
Over the Rainbow	*The Wizard of Oz*	84
Part of Your World	*The Little Mermaid*	88
The Pink Panther.	*The Pink Panther*	92
Raiders March	*Indiana Jones*	98
The Rainbow Connection	*The Muppet Movie*	102
Raindrops Keep Fallin' on My Head	*Butch Cassidy and the Sundance Kid*	95
(We're Gonna) Rock Around the Clock	*Blackboard Jungle*	106
The Rose	*The Rose*	108
Singin' in the Rain	*Singin' in the Rain*	111
Somewhere My Love	*Doctor Zhivago*	114
Star Wars® (Main Title)	*Star Wars*.	118
Stayin' Alive	*Saturday Night Fever*	120
Streets of Philadelphia	*Philadelphia*.	124
Take My Breath Away.	*Top Gun*	130
Under the Sea	*The Little Mermaid*	134
A Whole New World	*Aladdin*	127
The Wind Beneath My Wings	*Beaches*.	142
The Windmills of Your Mind	*The Thomas Crown Affair*	138

The 2002 film adaptation of the Kander and Ebb musical *Chicago* starred Renée Zellweger, Catherine Zeta Jones, Richard Gere, Queen Latifah, and Taye Diggs, to name a few. It won six Academy Awards and took home Best Picture of the Year for 2003. The last musical film to receive such a high honor was *Oliver!* (1968). A highlight of the movie is Zeta Jones' powerful performance of "And All That Jazz."

AND ALL THAT JAZZ

Chicago

Lyrics by Fred Ebb
Music by John Kander

13 G7 ... A♭7

Start the car,— I know a whoop - ee spot— where the gin is cold— but the pi -
Hold on, hon,— we're gon - na bun - ny hug,— I bought some as - pi - rin— down at U -

mf

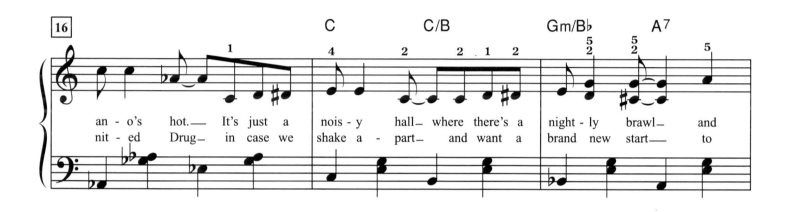

16 C · C/B · Gm/B♭ · A7

an - o's hot.— It's just a nois - y hall— where there's a night - ly brawl— and
nit - ed Drug— in case we shake a - part— and want a brand new start— to

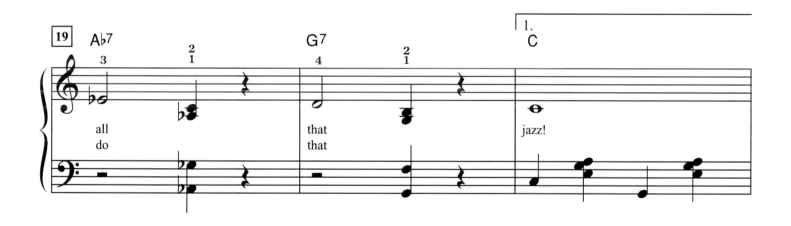

19 A♭7 · G7 · **1.** C

all that jazz!
do that

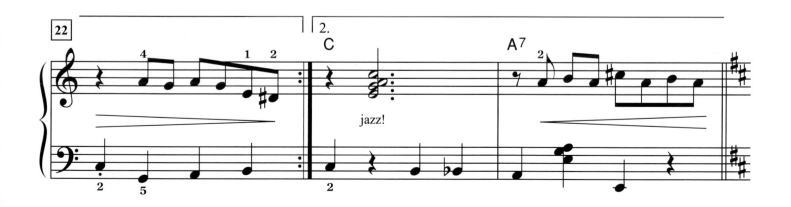

22 · **2.** C · A7

jazz!

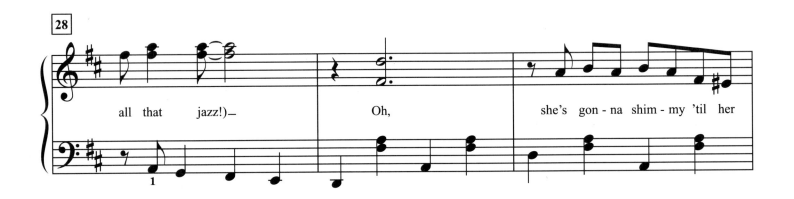

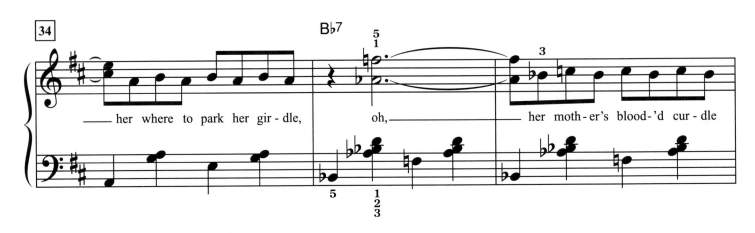

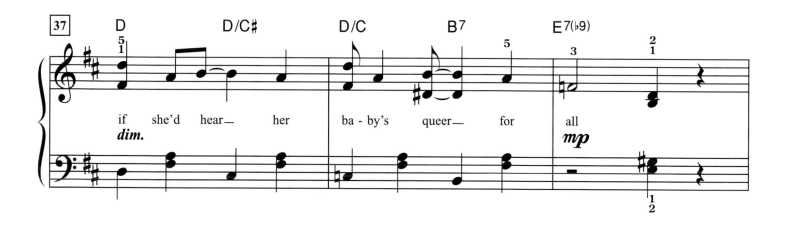

if she'd hear— her ba-by's queer— for all

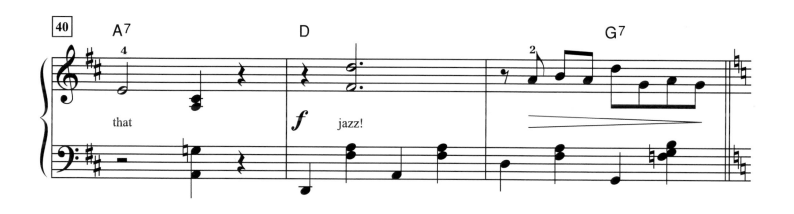

that jazz!

Find a flask,— we're play-ing fast and loose— and all that jazz!—

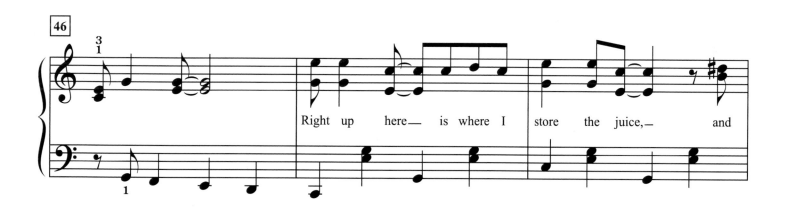

Right up here— is where I store the juice,— and

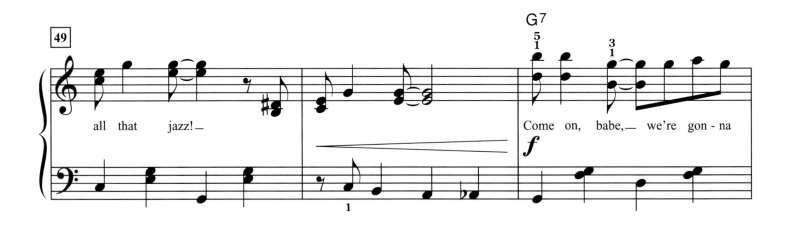

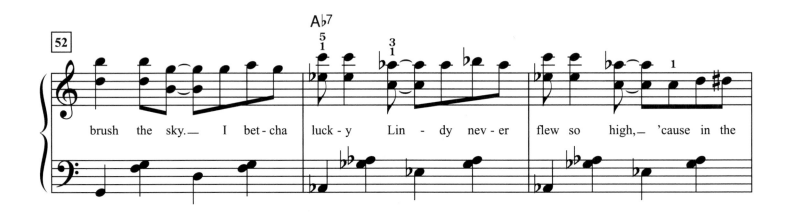

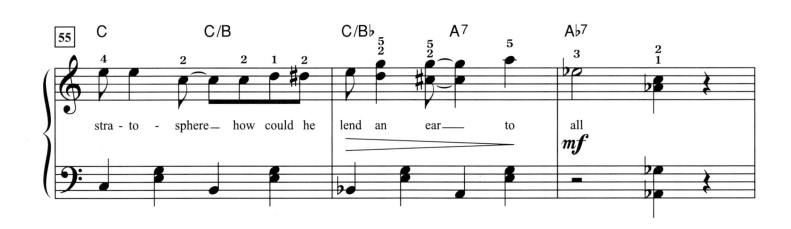

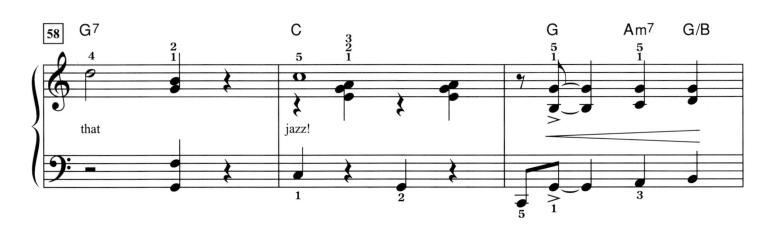

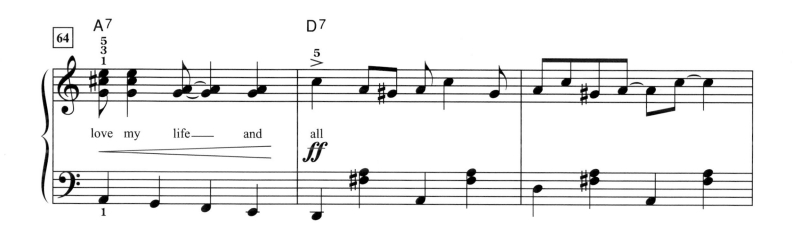

The powerhouse quartet of Burt Bacharach, Carole Bayer Sager, Christopher Cross and Peter Allen penned this famous song for the 1981 film *Arthur* starring Dudley Moore and Liza Minelli. In addition to box office success, the song garnered both an Academy Award and a Golden Globe for Best Original Song.

Arthur's Theme (Best That You Can Do)

Arthur

Words and Music by
Burt Bacharach, Carole Bayer Sager,
Christopher Cross and Peter Allen

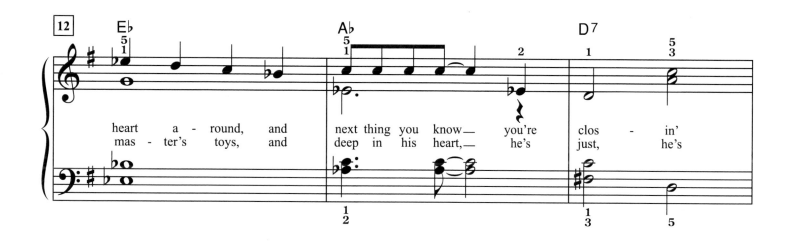

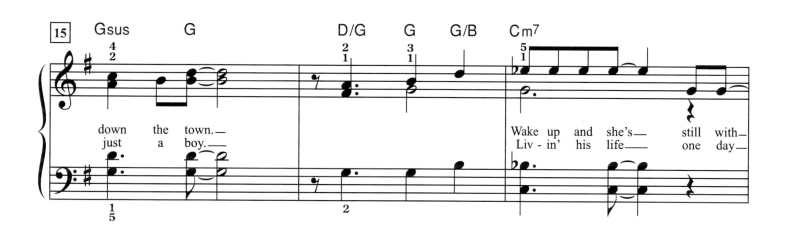

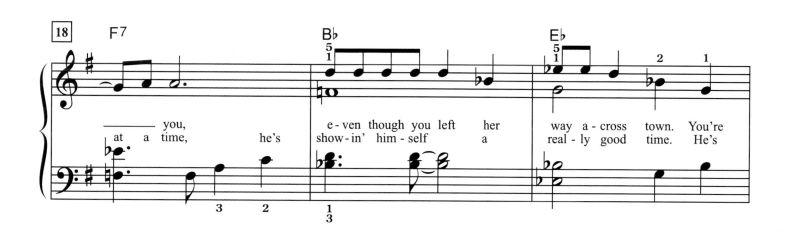

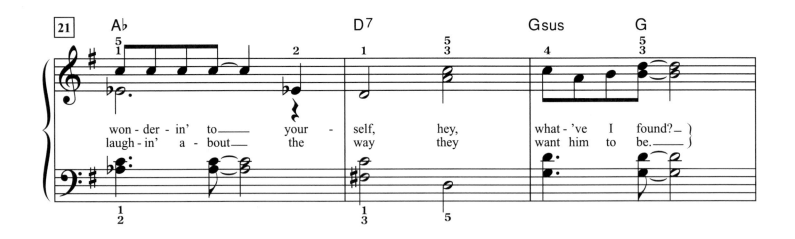

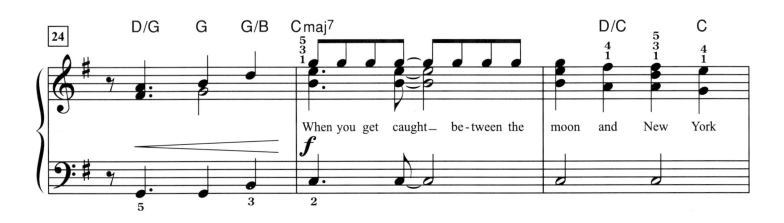

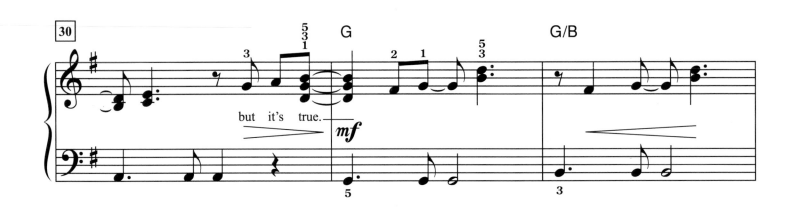

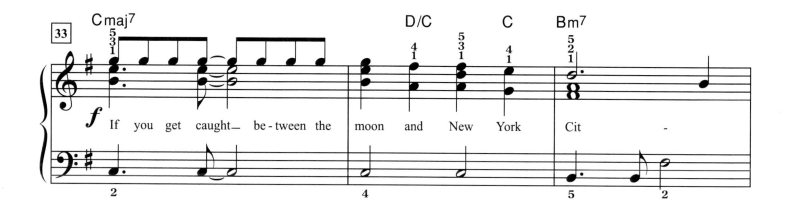

If you get caught— be-tween the moon and New York Cit -

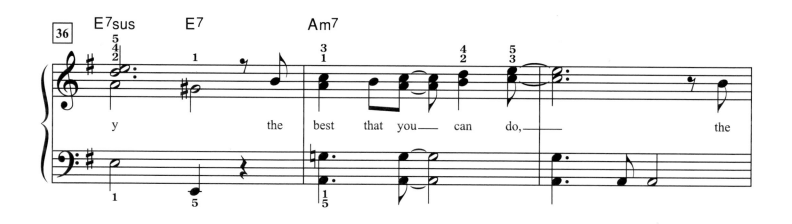

y the best that you— can do,— the

best that you— can do— is fall— in love.—

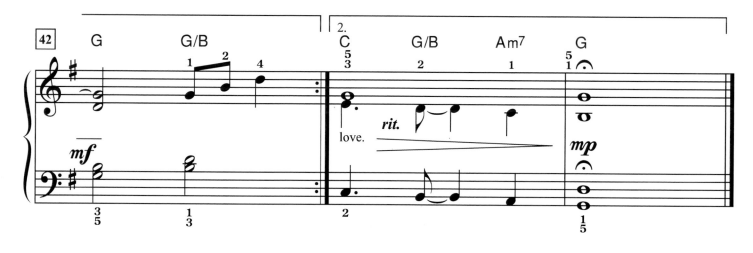

love.

In 1991 Walt Disney Pictures released *Beauty and the Beast,* an animated feature film based on the well-known fairy tale. It is the first and only animated film to be nominated for a Best Picture Academy Award. The story of *Beauty and the Beast* first appeared 250 years ago in a French book of children's stories by Jeanne-Marie de Beaumont.

BE OUR GUEST

Walt Disney's *Beauty and the Beast*

Words by Howard Ashman
Music by Alan Menken

Moderately, with spirit

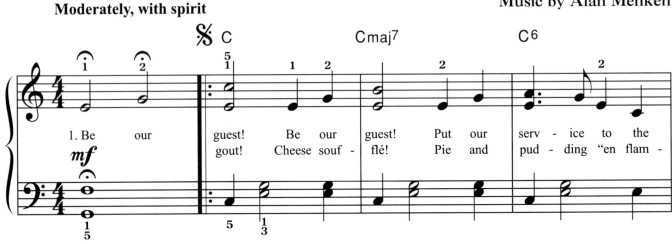

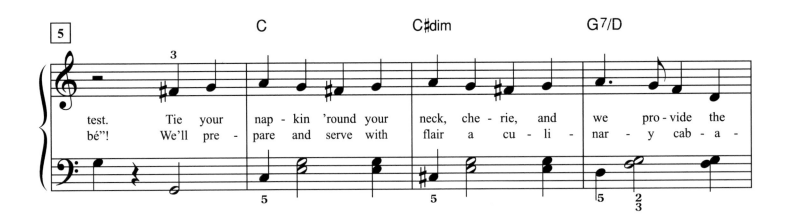

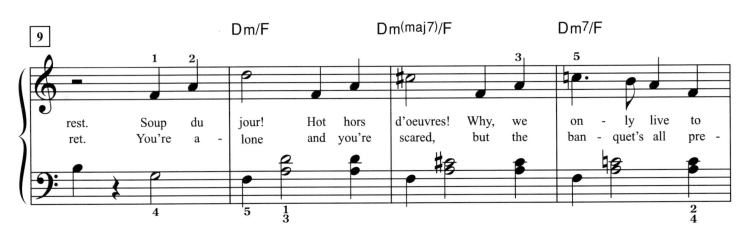

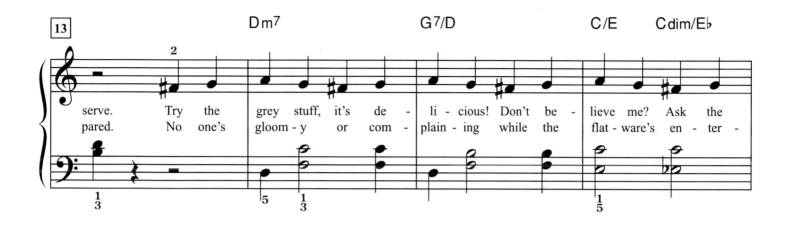

13 | Dm7 | | G7/D | | C/E | Cdim/E♭ |

serve. Try the grey stuff, it's de - li - cious! Don't be - lieve me? Ask the
pared. No one's gloom - y or com - plain - ing while the flat - ware's en - ter -

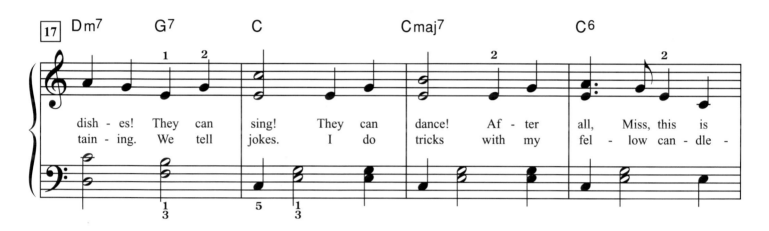

17 | Dm7 | G7 | C | Cmaj7 | C6 |

dish - es! They can sing! They can dance! Af - ter all, Miss, this is
tain - ing. We tell jokes. I do tricks with my fel - low can - dle -

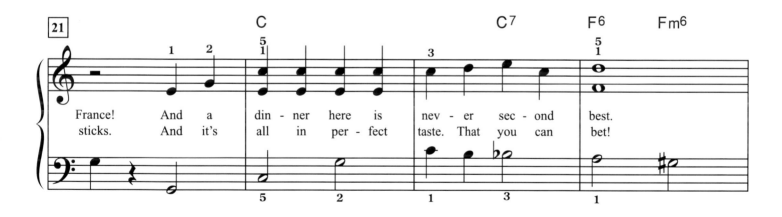

21 | | C | | C7 | F6 Fm6 |

France! And a din - ner here is nev - er sec - ond best.
sticks. And it's all in per - fect taste. That you can bet!

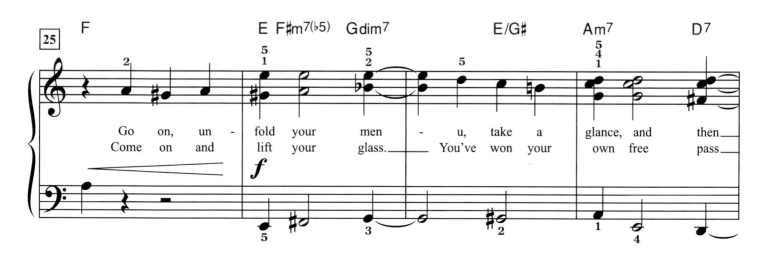

25 | F | E F#m7(♭5) Gdim7 | E/G# | Am7 | D7 |

Go on, un - fold your men - u, take a glance, and then
Come on and lift your glass. You've won your own free pass

f

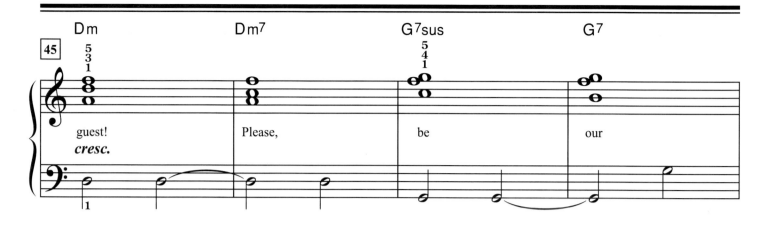

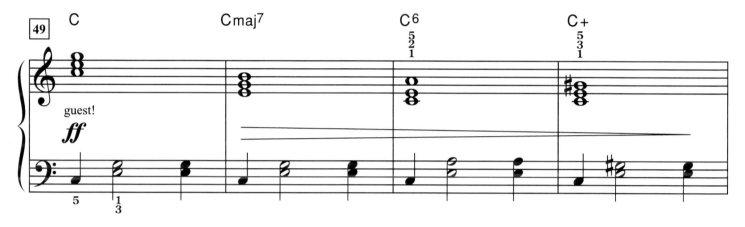

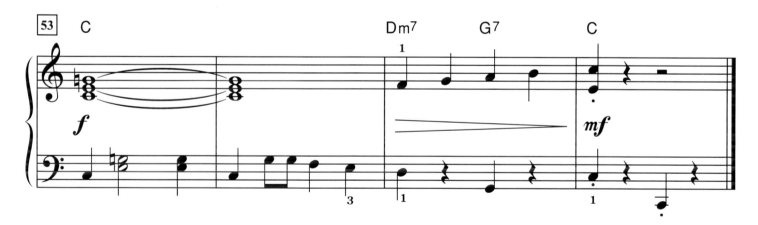

Verse 3:
Be our guest! Be our guest!
Our command is your request.
It's ten years since we had anybody here,
And we're obsessed.
With your meal, with your ease,
Yes, indeed, we aim to please,
While the candlelight's still glowing,
Let us help you, we'll keep going,
Course by course, one by one!
'Til you shout, "Enough, I'm done!"
Then we'll sing you off to sleep as you digest.
Tonight you'll prop your feet up!
But for now, let's eat up!
Be our guest!
Be our guest!
Be our guest!
Please, be our guest!

"Beauty and the Beast" is the leading single from the 1991 film and was sung in the movie by Angela Lansbury (as Mrs. Potts, the enchanted tea pot). Over the closing credits, Céline Dion and Peabo Bryson performed the song as a duet.

Beauty and the Beast

Walt Disney's *Beauty and the Beast*

Lyrics by Howard Ashman
Music by Alan Menken

Slowly, with expression

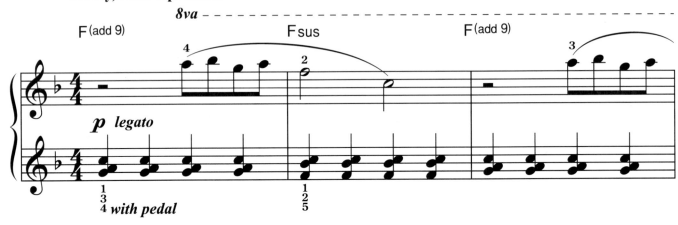

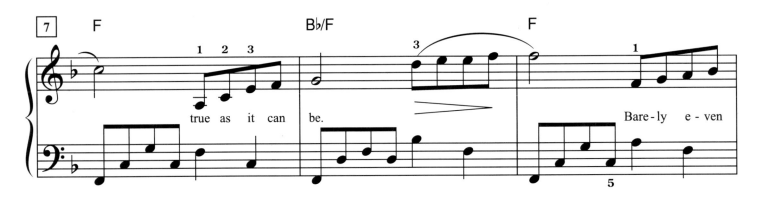

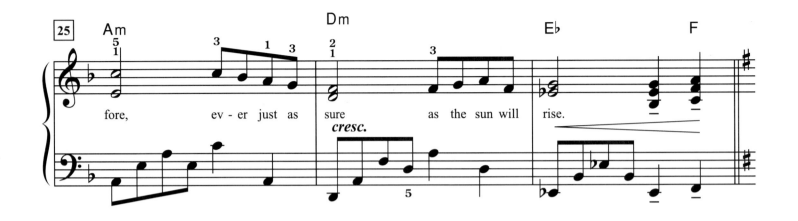

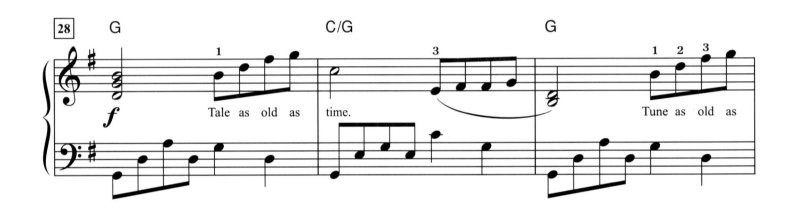

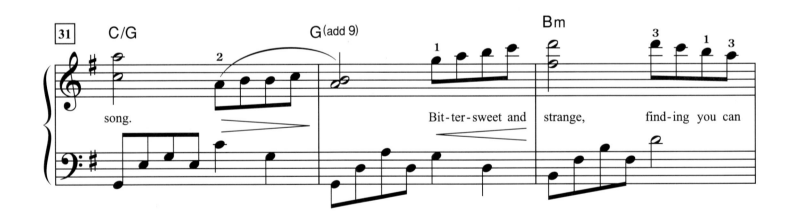

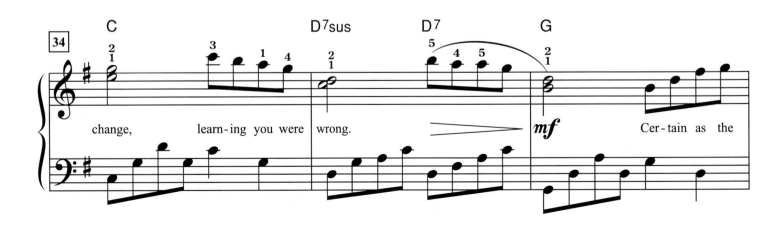

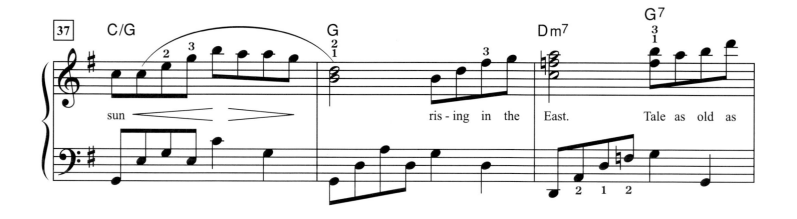

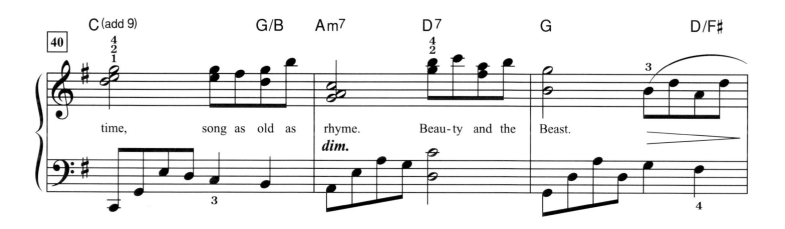

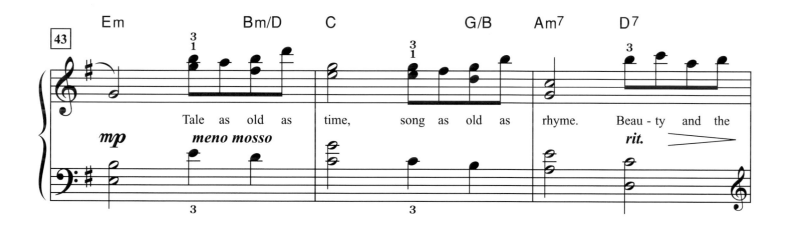

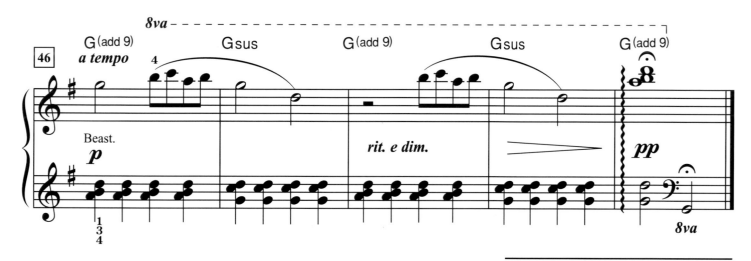

The 2004 Academy Award nominated film *The Polar Express* was based on the 1986 children's book by Chris Van Allsburg. "Believe," sung by Josh Groban and featured in various scenes throughout the movie, was nominated for Best Original Song at the Academy Awards and won a Grammy Award in 2006.

BELIEVE

The Polar Express

Words and Music by
Alan Silvestri and Glenn Ballard

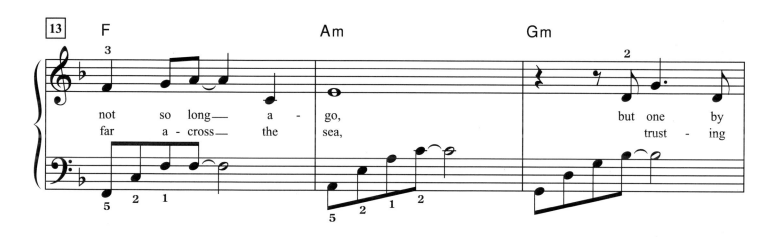

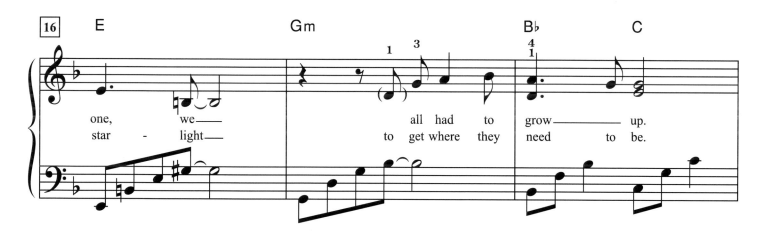

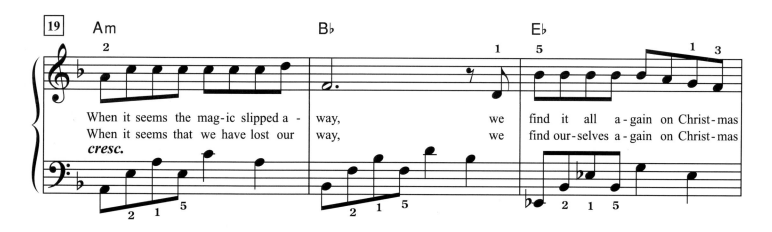

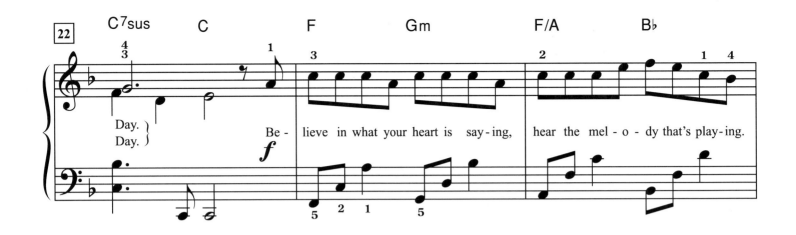

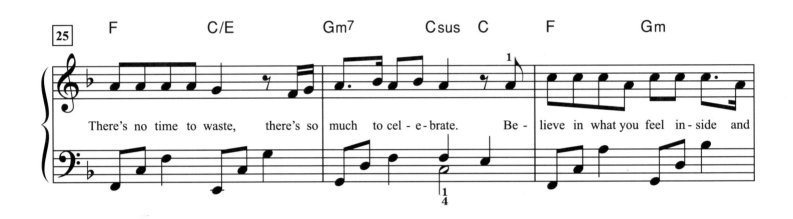

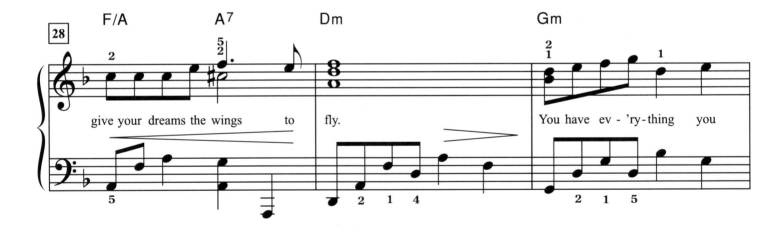

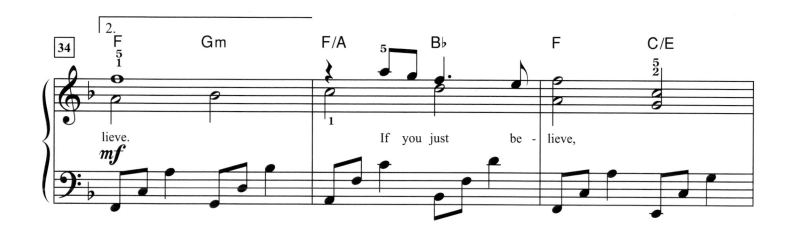

"As Time Goes By" was first composed for the little-known musical *Everybody's Welcome* (1931). However, its usage throughout the classic, romantic film *Casablanca* (1942) made it famous. *Casablanca* starred Humphrey Bogart as Rick, a conflicted nightclub owner, and Ingrid Bergman as Ilsa, Rick's former lover. "As Time Goes By" was "their song" and was performed in the film by Dooley Wilson who played Sam, Rick's nightclub pianist. *Casablanca* won three Academy Awards in 1943, including Best Picture.

AS TIME GOES BY

Casablanca

Words and Music by
Herman Hupfeld

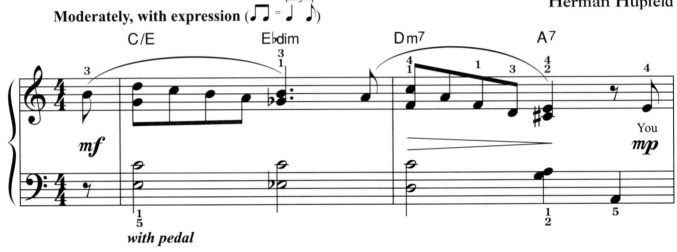

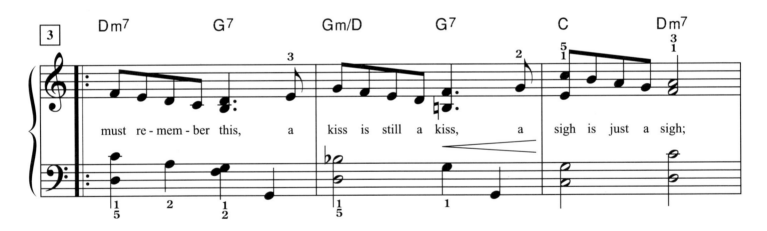

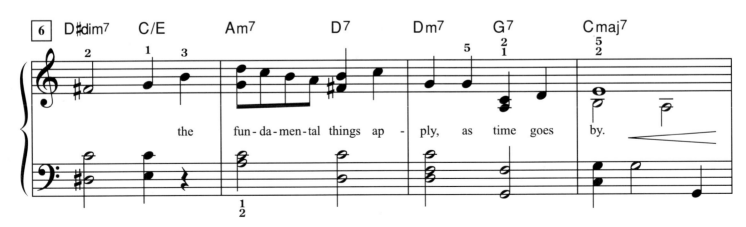

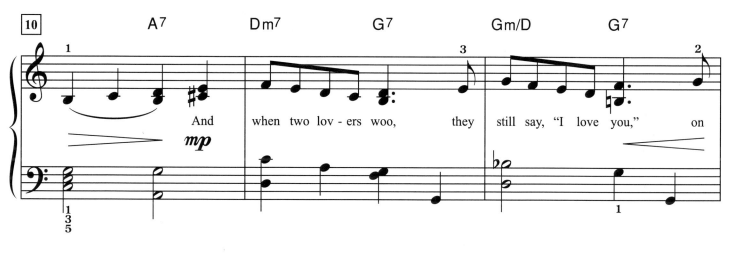

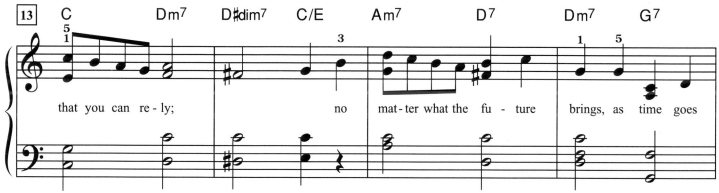

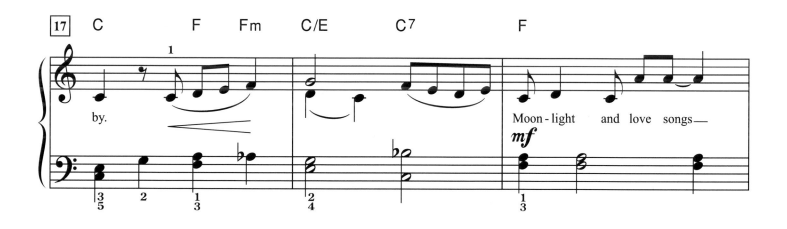

The Lion King (1994) is Walt Disney's 32nd animated feature film and one of the highest-grossing animated films in history. The film won two Academy Awards: Best Original Score (Hans Zimmer) and Best Original Song for "Can You Feel the Love Tonight" (Elton John and Tim Rice). Elton John performed "Can You Feel the Love Tonight" for the closing credits of the film and won a Grammy Award for the performance.

CAN YOU FEEL THE LOVE TONIGHT

Walt Disney's *The Lion King*

Music by Elton John
Words by Tim Rice

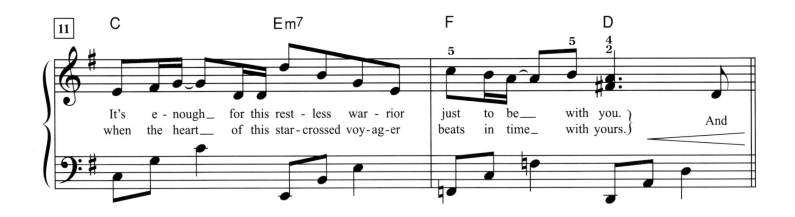

It's e-nough_ for this rest-less war-rior just to be__ with you. And
when the heart__ of this star-crossed voy-ag-er beats in time_ with yours.

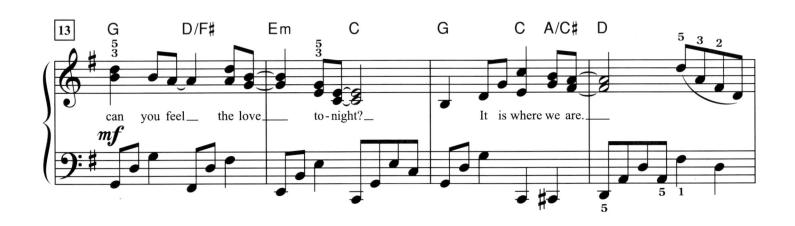

can you feel_ the love_ to-night?_ It is where we are.__

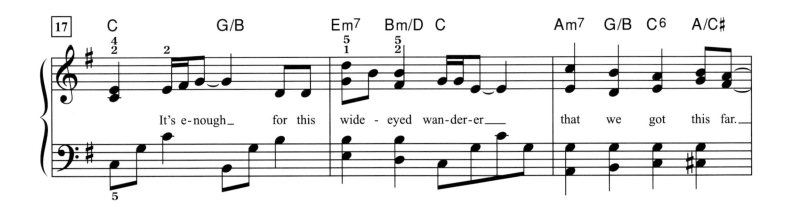

It's e-nough_ for this wide-eyed wan-der-er__ that we got this far.

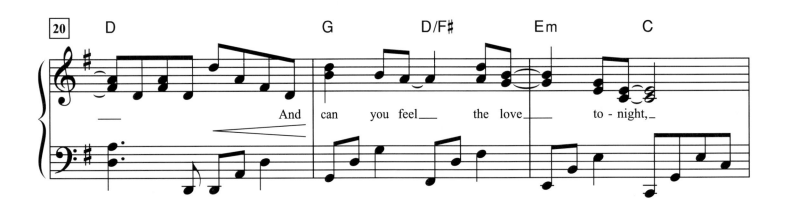

__ And can you feel__ the love__ to-night,_

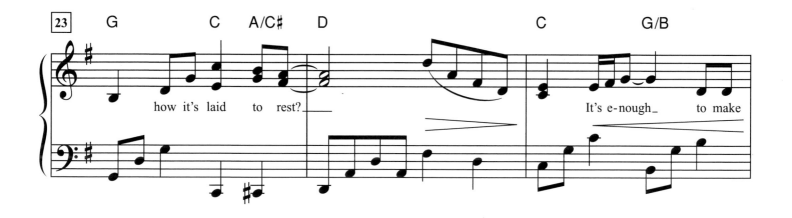

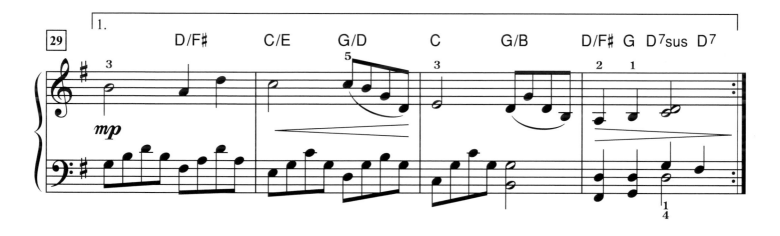

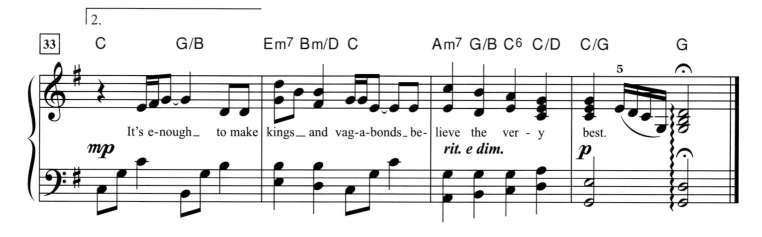

Blake Edwards directed Jack Lemmon and Lee Remick in the 1962 Academy Award-winning film *The Days of Wine and Roses*, a story about a couple that faces alcoholism. The Best Original Song was written by Henry Mancini with lyrics by Johnny Mercer. The phrase "days of wine and roses" is originally from a poem by a late-19th century English poet, Ernest Dowson.

THE DAYS OF WINE AND ROSES

The Days of Wine and Roses

Lyric by Johnny Mercer
Music by Henry Mancini

"Colors of the Wind" is the Oscar-winning Best Original Song from Walt Disney's *Pocahontas* (1995). In the film, Pocahontas (as sung by Judy Kuhn), the beautiful Native American princess, sings this song to convince British explorer John Smith of the wisdom of her people—of mankind's connection to nature. Vanessa Williams recorded the song for the end credits. Released as a single, the song reached #4 on the Billboard Hot 100, and the movie's soundtrack reached #1 on the Billboard 200.

Colors of the Wind

Walt Disney's *Pocahontas*

Lyrics by Stephen Schwartz
Music by Alan Menken

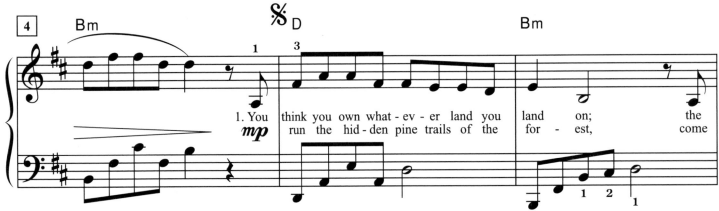

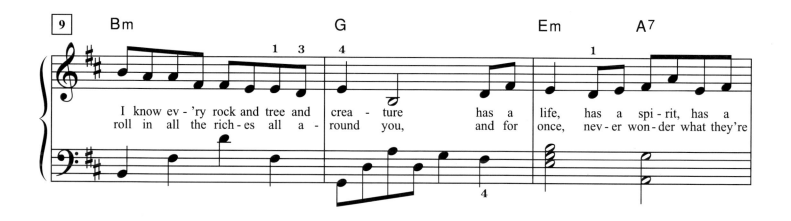

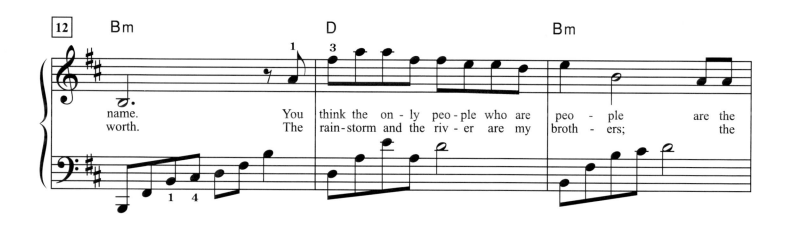

to Coda ⊕

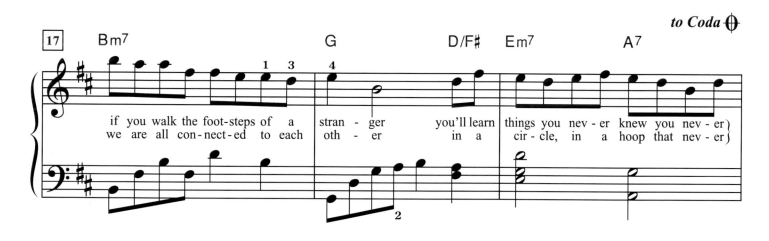

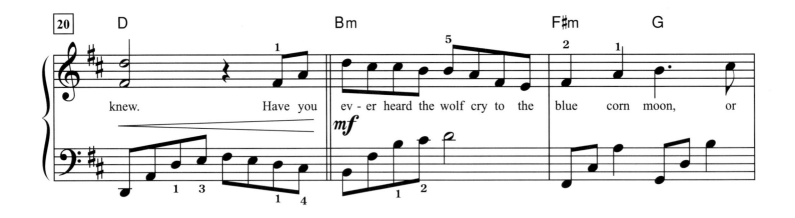

knew. Have you ev - er heard the wolf cry to the blue corn moon, or

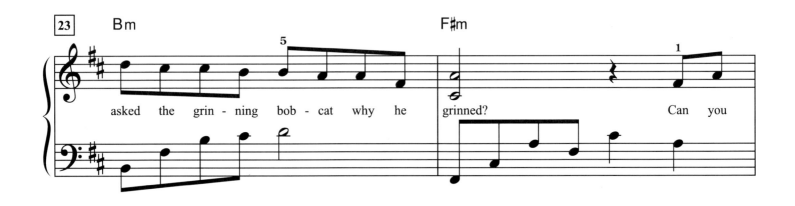

asked the grin - ning bob - cat why he grinned? Can you

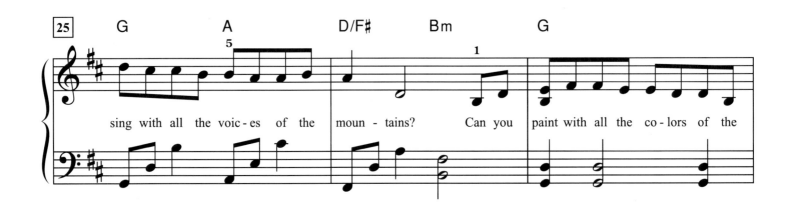

sing with all the voic - es of the moun - tains? Can you paint with all the co - lors of the

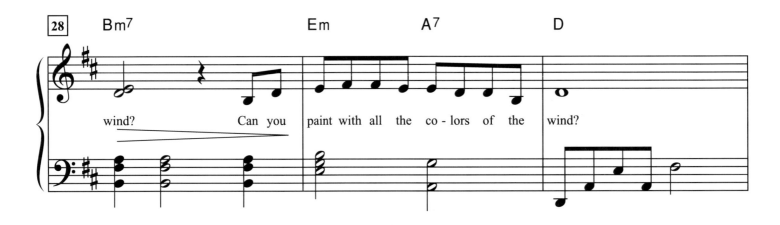

wind? Can you paint with all the co - lors of the wind?

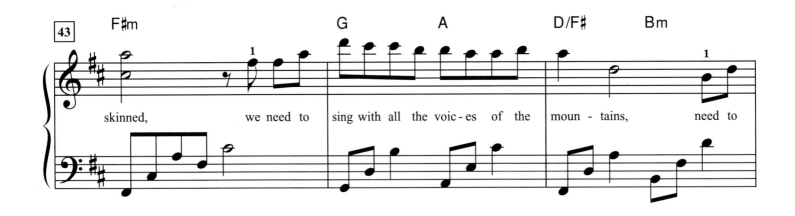

skinned, we need to sing with all the voic-es of the moun-tains, need to

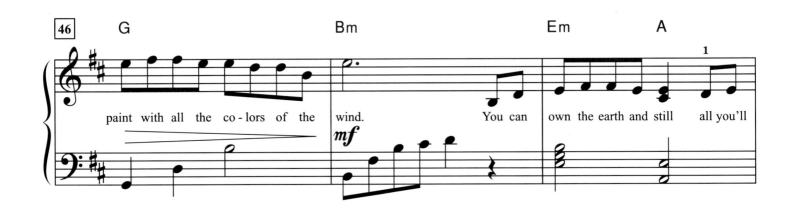

paint with all the co-lors of the wind. You can own the earth and still all you'll

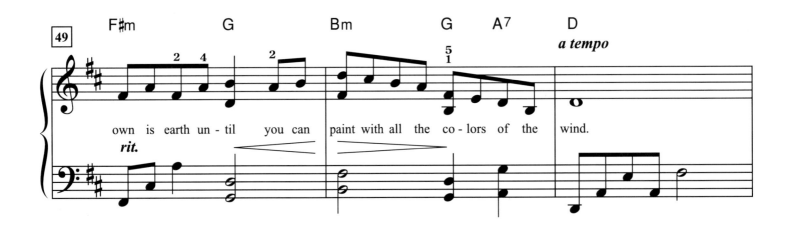

own is earth un-til you can paint with all the co-lors of the wind.

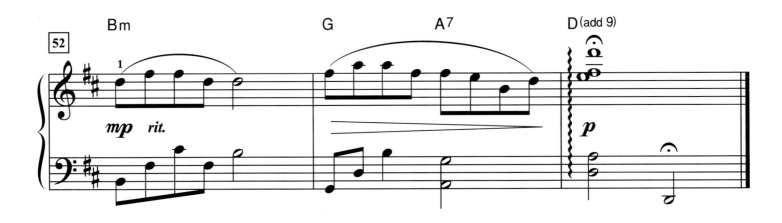

Soul singer Diana Ross and pop singer Lionel Richie recorded "Endless Love" in 1981 for the romantic drama of the same name. The movie was directed by Franco Zeffirelli and starred Brooke Shields and Martin Hewitt. The film was a commercial failure, but the song became the biggest-selling single of the year and has become one of the most popular duet ballads of all time. It was covered by Luther Vandross and Mariah Carey in 1994.

ENDLESS LOVE
Endless Love

Words and Music by
Lionel Richie

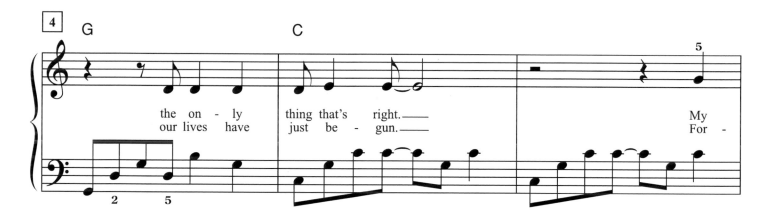

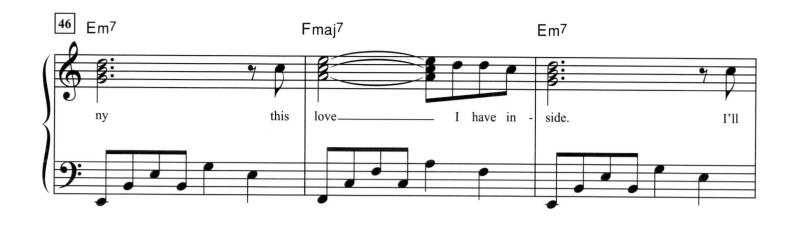

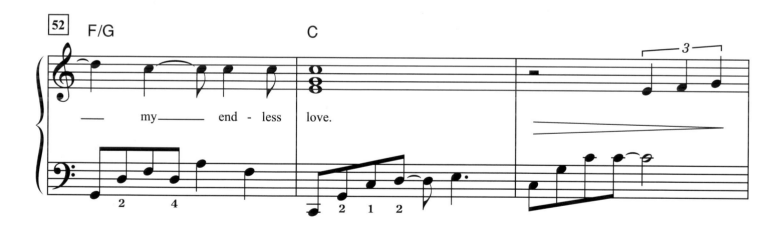

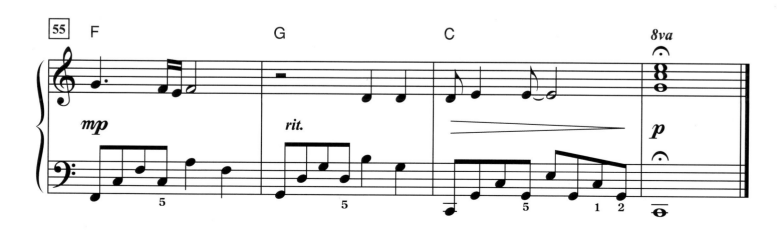

"Evergreen" was a worldwide success in 1976, peaking at #1 on the Billboard Hot 100 and winning Academy, Grammy, and Golden Globe awards. It was performed by Barbra Streisand for the film *A Star Is Born*, starring Streisand and Kris Kristofferson. It is a story about a couple whose unequally successful singing careers create drama in their relationship. The movie is a remake of two earlier versions—one starring Janet Gaynor (1937) and one starring Judy Garland (1954).

EVERGREEN

A Star Is Born

Words by Paul Williams
Music by Barbra Streisand

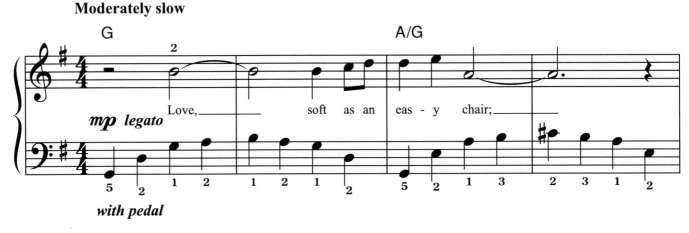

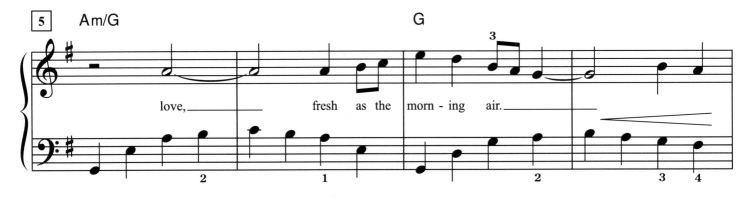

Sylvester Stallone asked the rock band Survivor to write a theme song for *Rocky III* (1982), the third of six movies about a boxer from Philadelphia. "Eye of the Tiger" was the result and became a smash hit, topping the Billboard Hot 100 for six weeks and winning a Grammy Award. The title of the hard rock anthem was based on a line from the movie's script, written by Stallone.

Eye of the Tiger

Rocky III

Words and Music by
Frankie Sullivan III and Jim Peterik

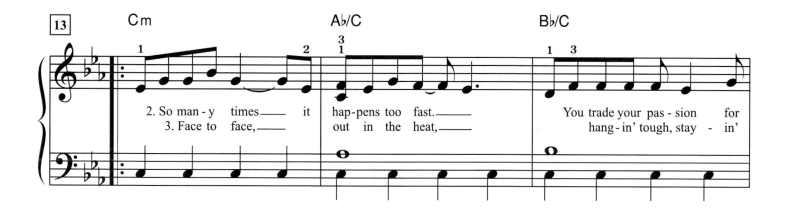

13 Cm / Ab/C / Bb/C

2. So man - y times ___ it hap-pens too fast. ___ You trade your pas - sion for
3. Face to face, ___ out in the heat, ___ hang - in' tough, stay - in'

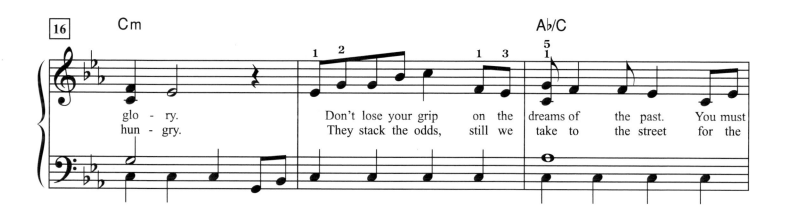

16 Cm / Ab/C

glo - ry. Don't lose your grip on the dreams of the past. You must
hun - gry. They stack the odds, still we take to the street for the

19 Bb/C / Cm / Bb Cm Fm

fight just to keep them a - live. It's the eye of the ti - ger. It's the
kill with the will to sur - vive.

f

22 Eb/G / Bb Cm Fm / Cm Bb Cm

thrill of the fight, ris - in' up to the chal - lenge of our ri - val. And the

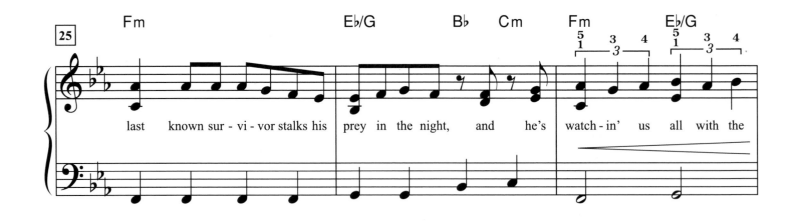

last known sur - vi - vor stalks his prey in the night, and he's watch - in' us all with the

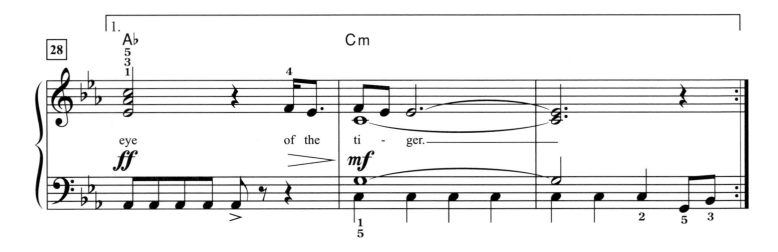

eye of the ti - ger.

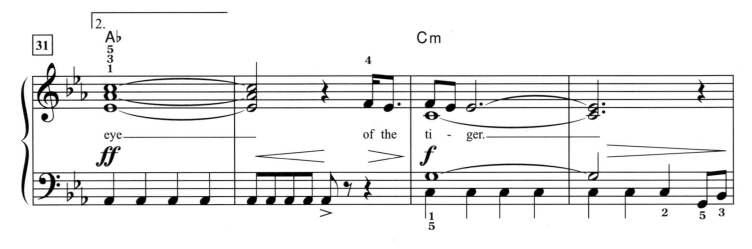

eye of the ti - ger.

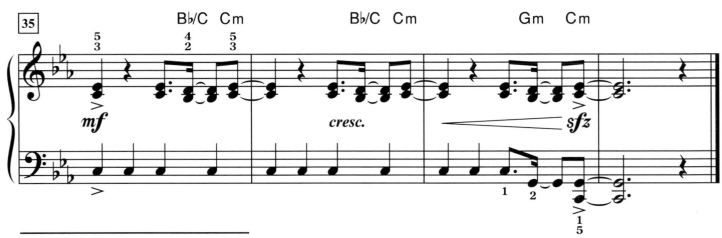

"Georgy Girl" is the title song from the 1966 British film of the same name. The movie was nominated for two Academy Awards: Best Original Song (as performed by The Seekers, an Australian band) and Best Actress (Lynn Redgrave in the title role). The song reached the top of the charts in the U.S., Australia, and Great Britain.

GEORGY GIRL

Georgy Girl

Words by Jim Dale
Music by Tom Springfield

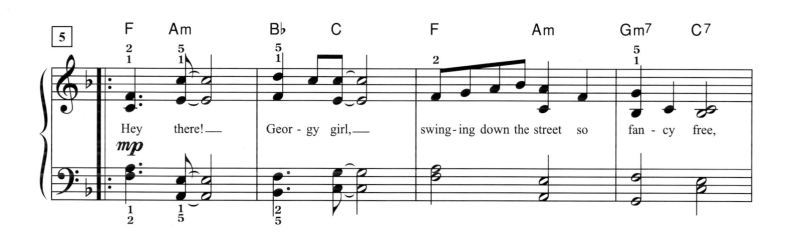

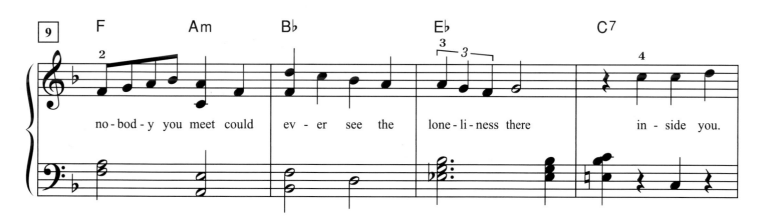

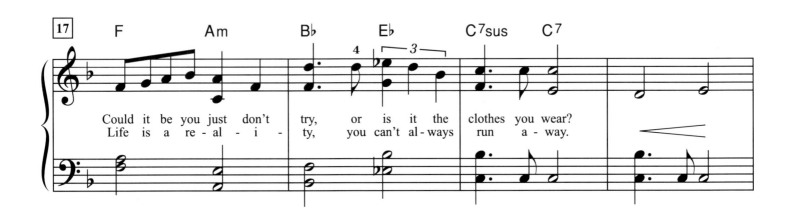

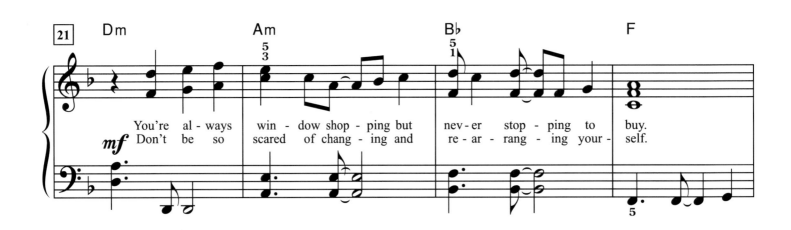

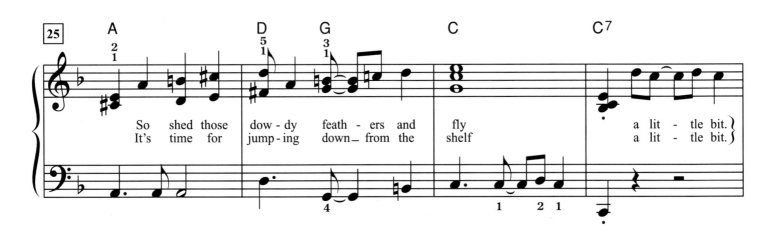

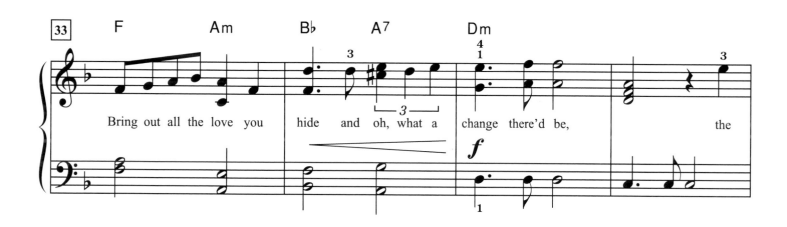

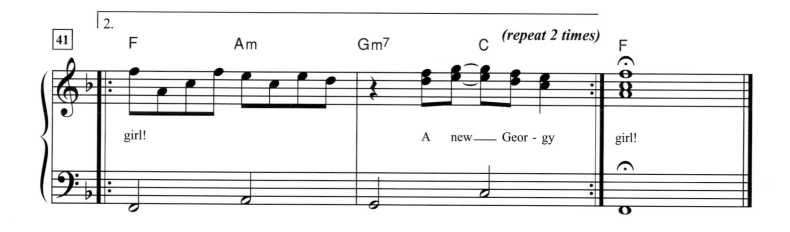

Fame is a 1980 musical film about students at the New York High School of Performing Arts. The music from the film was critically successful; "Fame" won the Academy Award and Golden Globe Award for Best Original Song, and the score won an Academy Award as well. Irene Cara, who played Coco Hernandez in the film, recorded "Fame" as well as "Out Here on My Own," another single from the soundtrack which was also nominated for an Academy Award.

FAME

Fame

Music by Michael Gore
Lyrics by Dean Pitchford

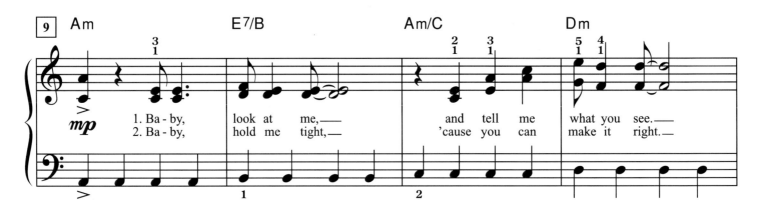

13 G ... D

You ain't seen the best of me yet.
You can shoot me straight to the top.

Give me time, I'll make
Give me love, and take

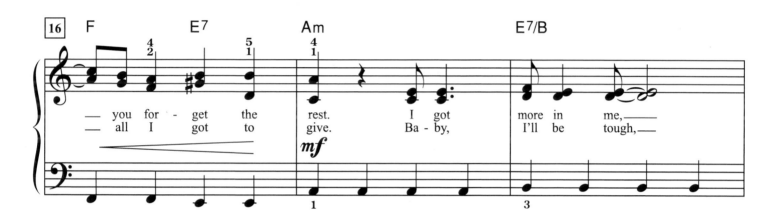

16 F E7 Am E7/B

you for - get the rest. I got
all I got to give. Ba - by,

more in me,
I'll be tough,

mf

19 Am/C Dm G

and you can set it free.
too much is not e - nough.

I can catch the moon
I can ride your heart

22 D E7

in my hand.
'til it breaks.

Don't you know who I
Ooh, I got what it

am?
takes.

Re - mem - ber my

cresc.

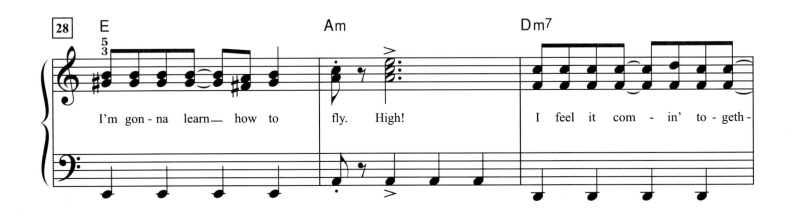

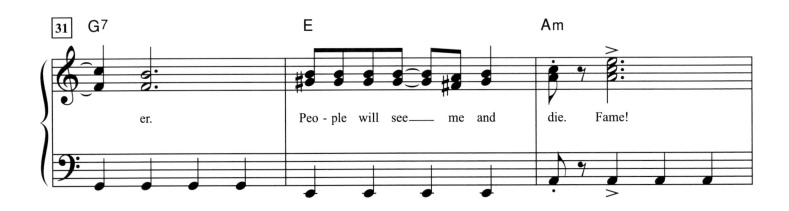

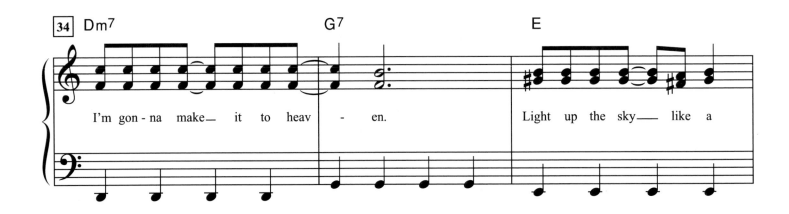

flame. Fame! I'm gon - na live—— for - ev - er.

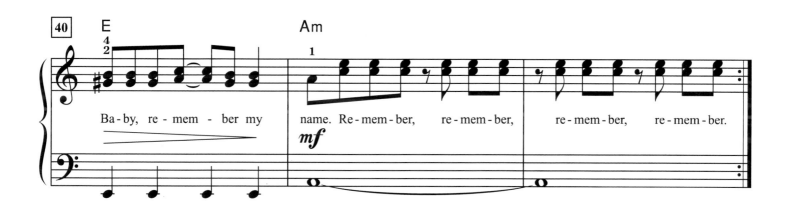

Ba - by, re - mem - ber my name. Re - mem - ber, re - mem - ber, re - mem - ber, re - mem - ber.

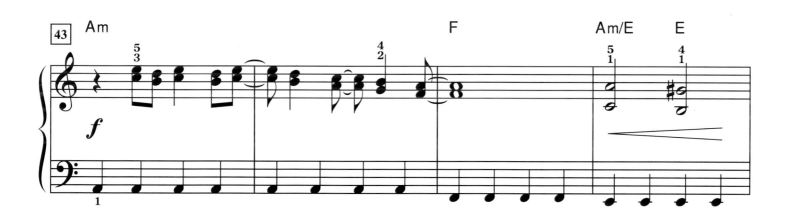

This famous movie theme accompanies Rocky Balboa (played by Sylvester Stallone), in the 1976 film *Rocky,* working through a rigorous training regimen which concludes with a sprint up the steps of the Philadelphia Museum of Art. "Gonna Fly Now" was nominated for an Academy Award and the recording reached number one on the Billboard Hot 100 chart in 1977.

Gonna Fly Now

Rocky

By Bill Conti, Ayn Robbins
and Carol Connors

With a steady, driving beat

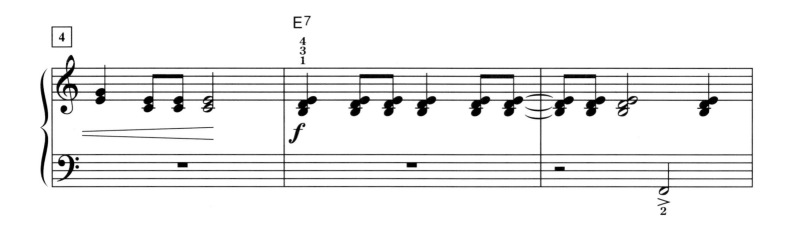

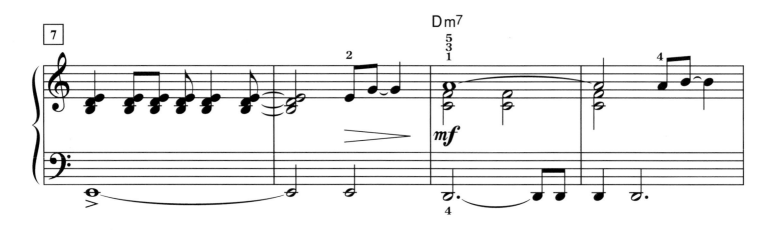

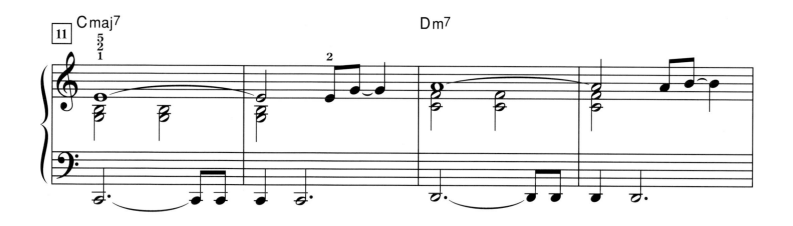

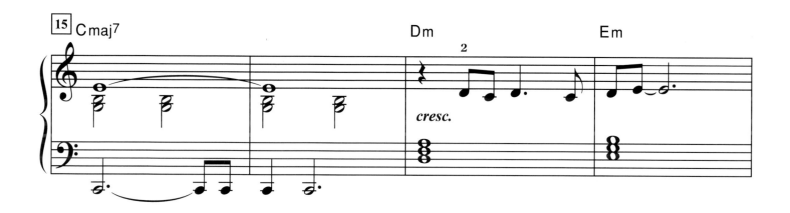

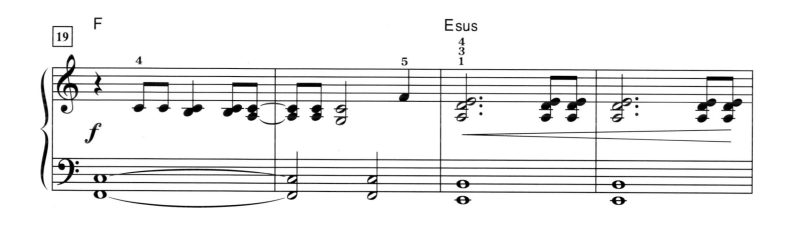

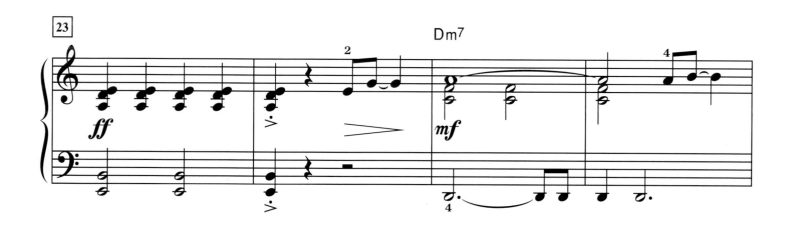

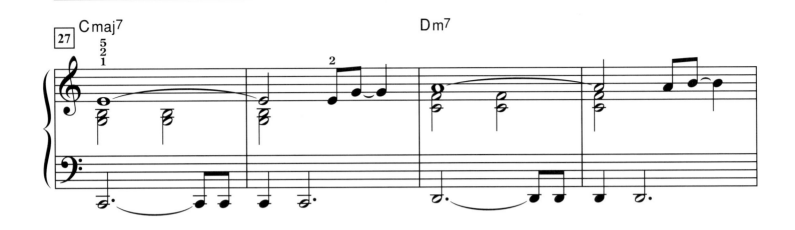

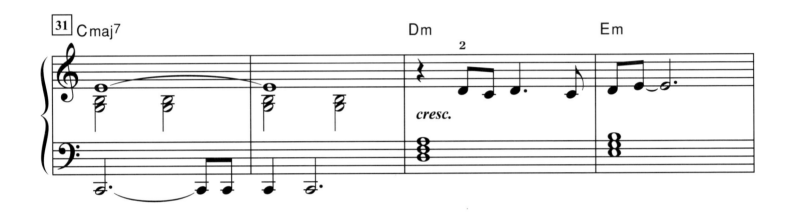

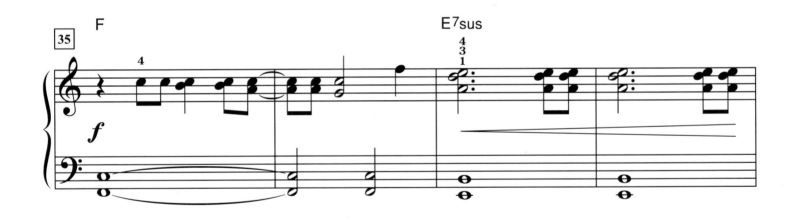

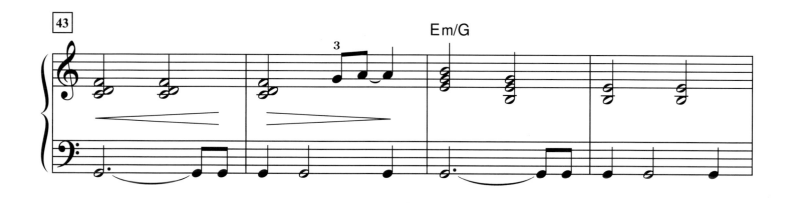

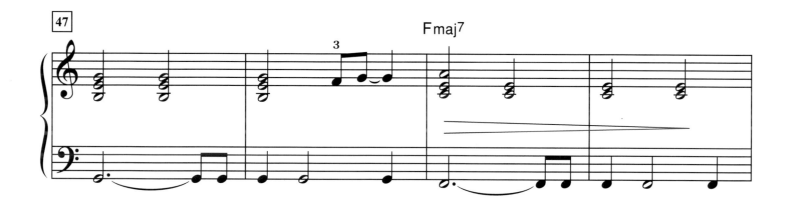

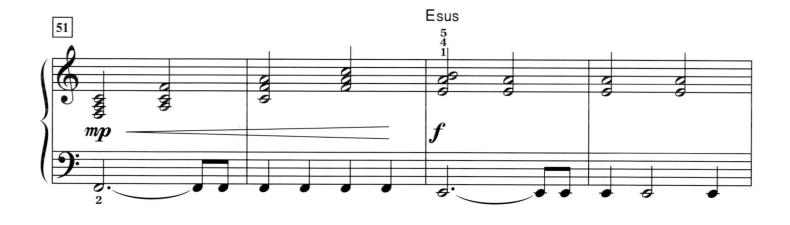

"Hedwig's Theme" is considered to be the main theme from the series of *Harry Potter* movies. It has been used in every film to date, even in the movies in which John Williams was not the sole composer. It was initially composed for the first movie in the Harry Potter film series, *Harry Potter and the Sorcerer's Stone*.

HEDWIG'S THEME
Harry Potter and the Sorcerer's Stone

By JOHN WILLIAMS

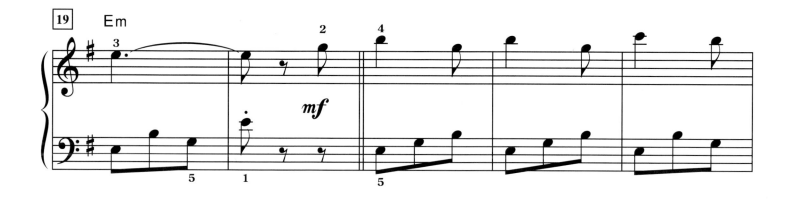

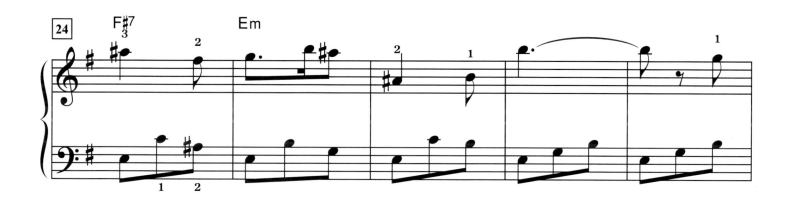

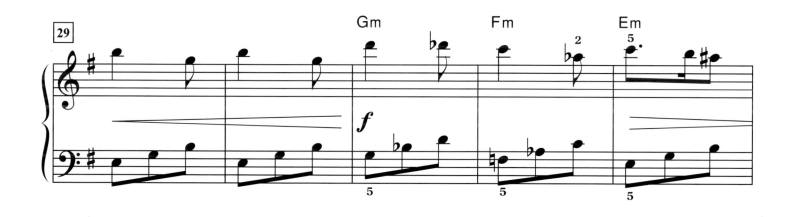

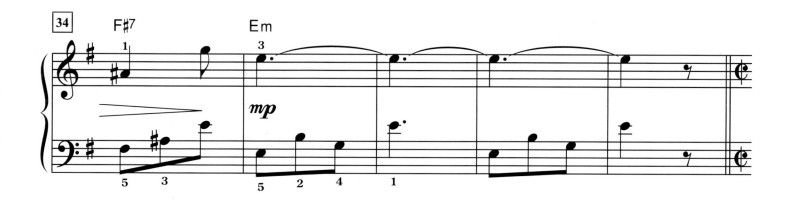

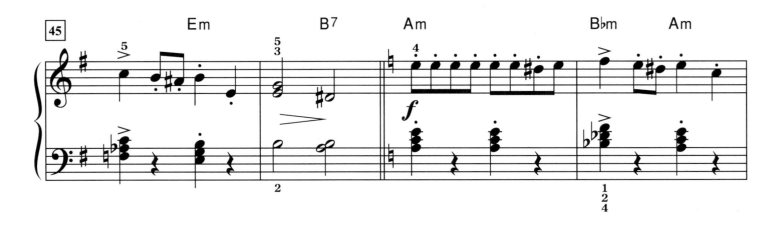

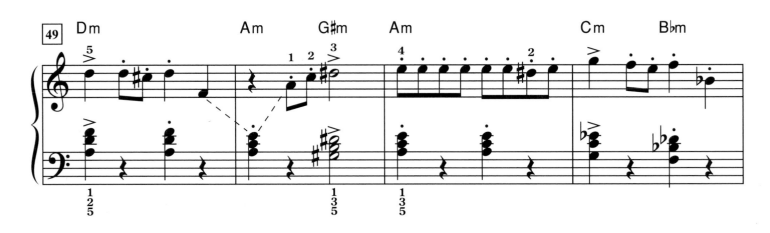

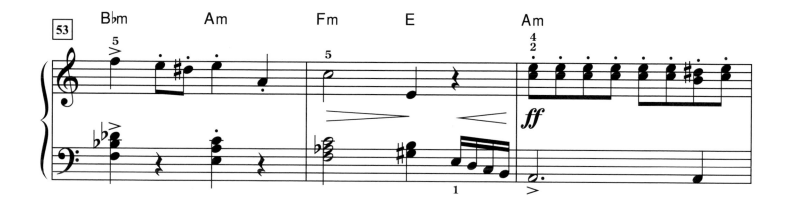

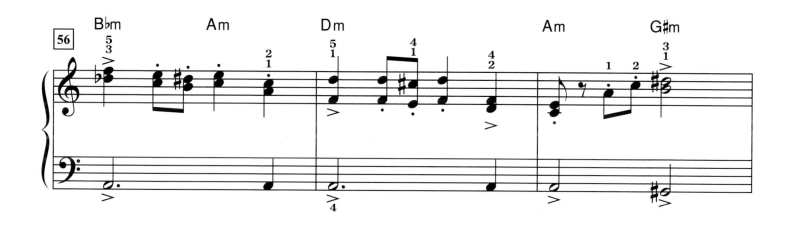

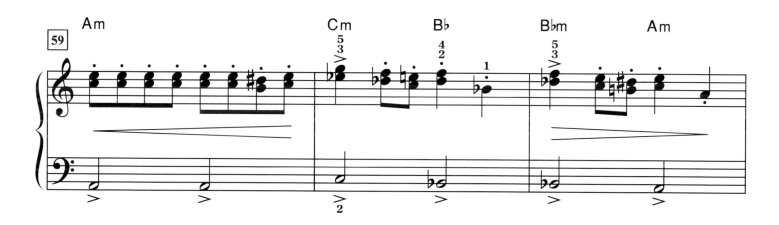

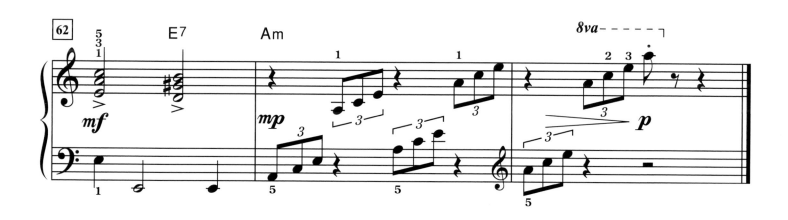

Aerosmith recorded the power ballad "I Don't Want to Miss a Thing" in 1998 for the sci-fi blockbuster *Armageddon*. The single debuted on the Billboard Hot 100 at #1, was nominated for an Academy Award, and introduced the band to a new generation of listeners.

I Don't Want to Miss a Thing

Armageddon

Words and Music by
Diane Warren

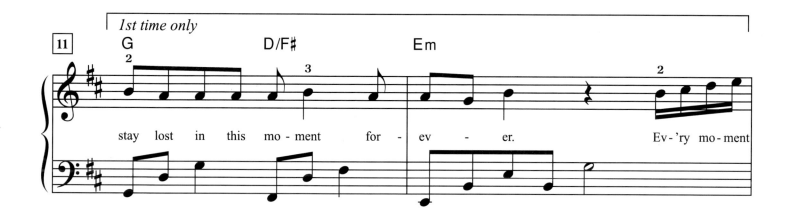

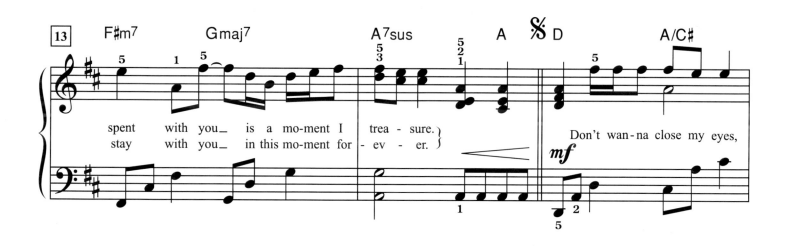

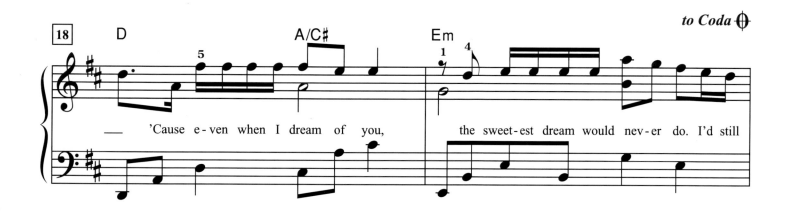

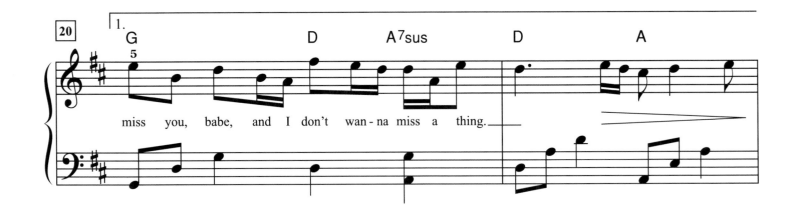

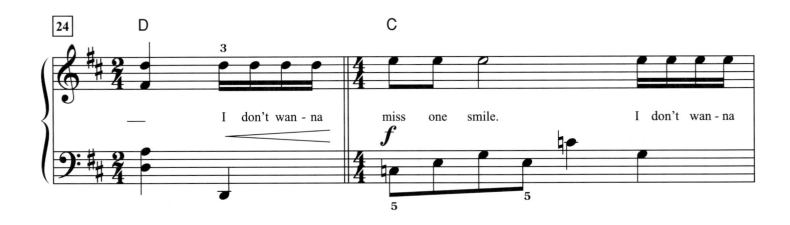

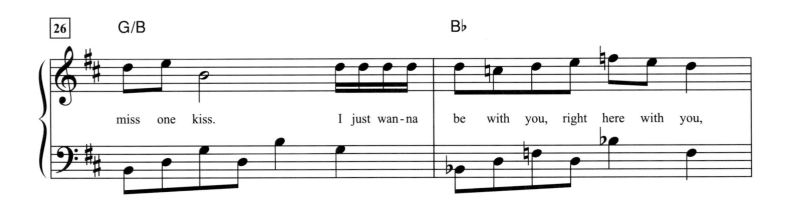

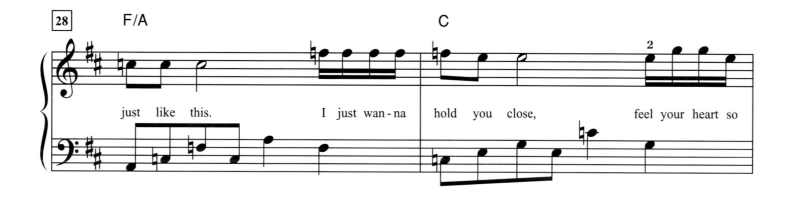

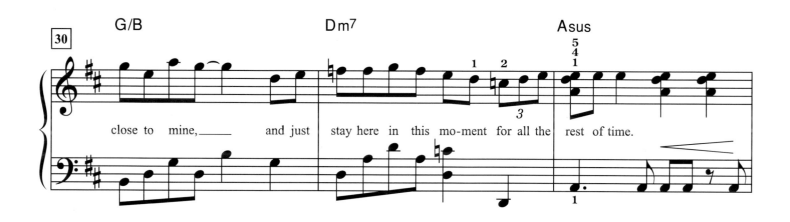

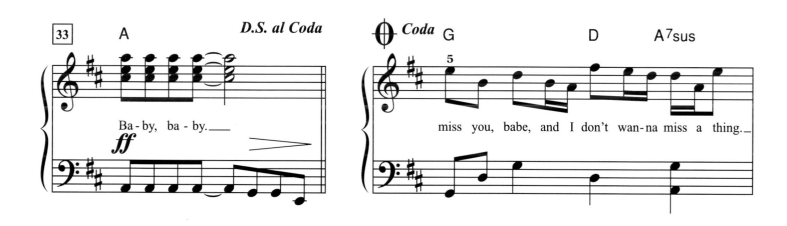

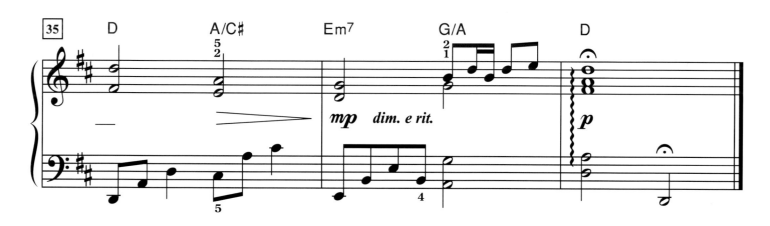

The Lord of the Rings: The Fellowship of the Ring is one of the highest grossing movies of all time. Since its 2001 release, two other films based on the J. R. R. Tolkien books have been made under the direction of Peter Jackson. The lyricist of "In Dreams," Fran Walsh, is also the life and business partner of Jackson.

In Dreams

The Lord of the Rings: The Fellowship of the Ring

Words and Music by
Fran Walsh and Howard Shore

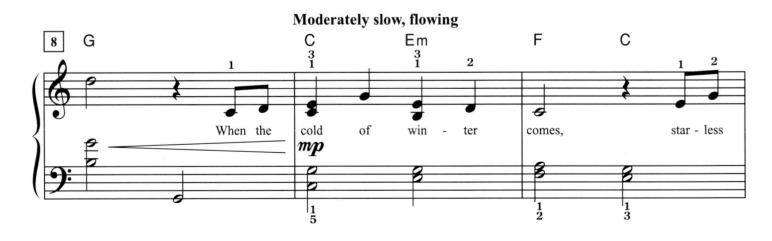

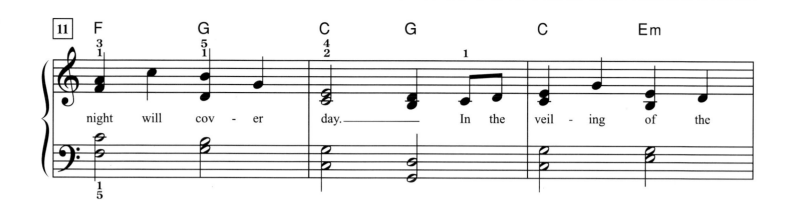

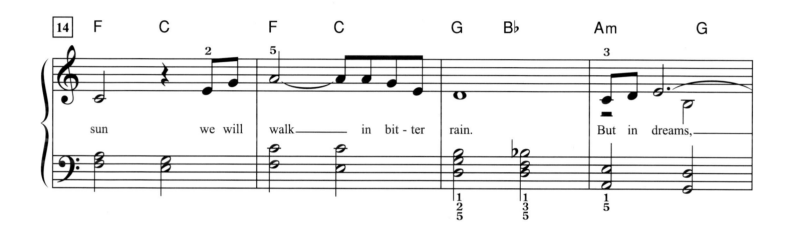

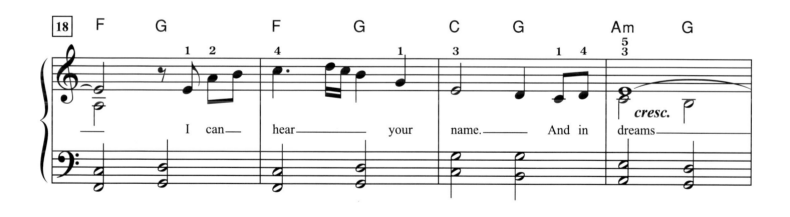

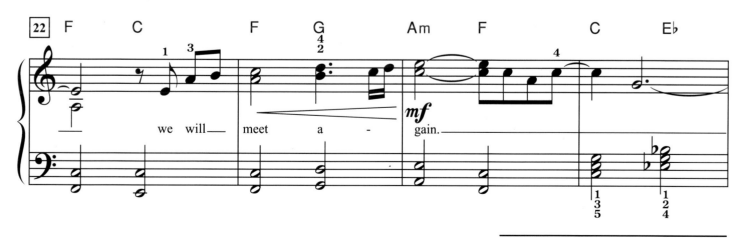

The "James Bond Theme" first appeared in 1962 in *Dr. No,* the first of the James Bond films. Since then the instrumentation has varied from electric guitar to symphony orchestra to Moog synthesizer and has had influences from disco to electronica. It evolved throughout the series and has reflected the lead character and the era of each movie.

JAMES BOND THEME

James Bond

Moderately bright

By Monty Norman

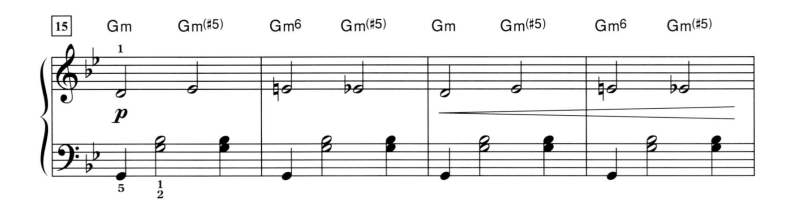

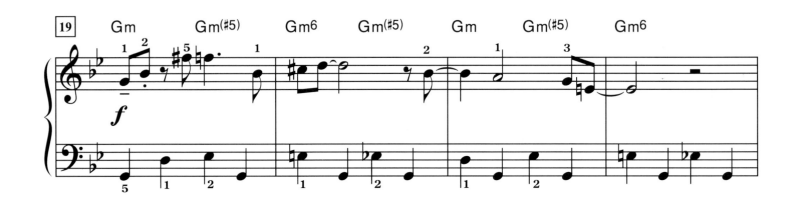

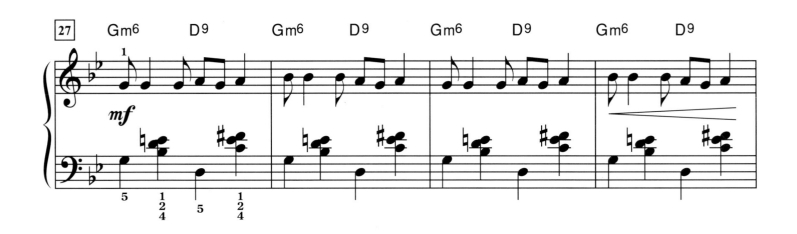

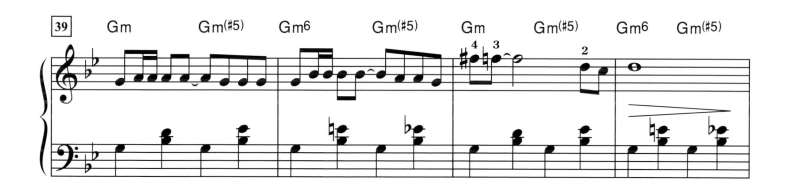

Laura (1944) is an Academy Award-winning film noir based on a popular 1943 detective novel by Vera Caspary. The film's brooding theme music was written by David Raksin, who composed it after he had unfortunately received a "Dear John" letter from his wife. Lyrics were added by Johnny Mercer, and the song has become a jazz standard having been recorded by hundreds of artists.

LAURA

Laura

Lyrics by Johnny Mercer
Music by David Raksin

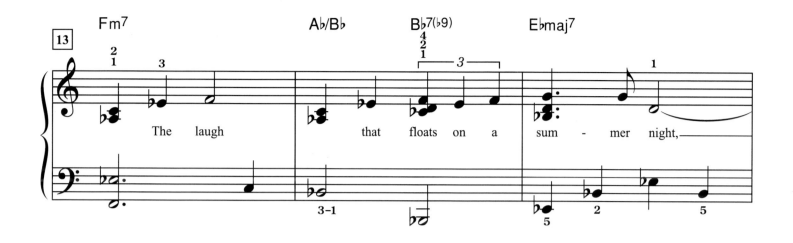

The laugh that floats on a sum - mer night,———

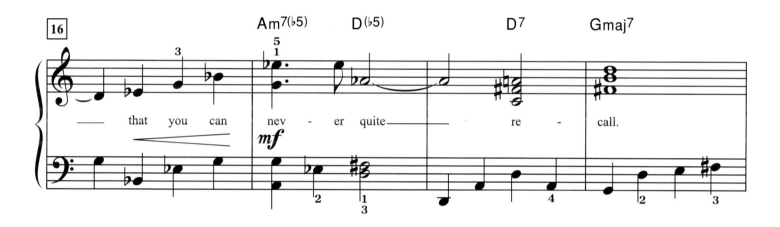

———— that you can nev - er quite—— re - call.

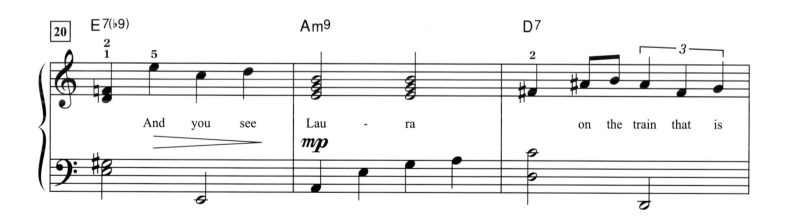

And you see Lau - ra on the train that is

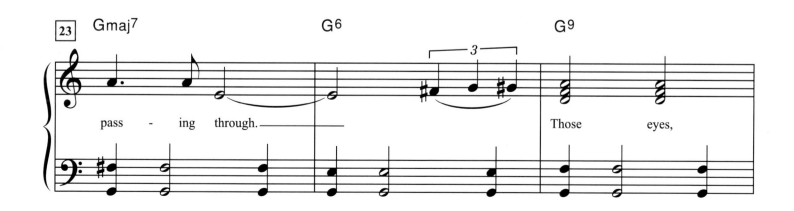

pass - ing through.——— Those eyes,

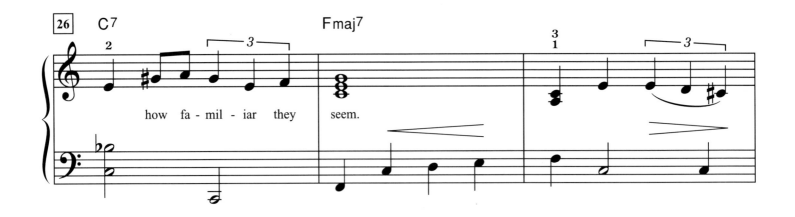

how fa - mil - iar they seem.

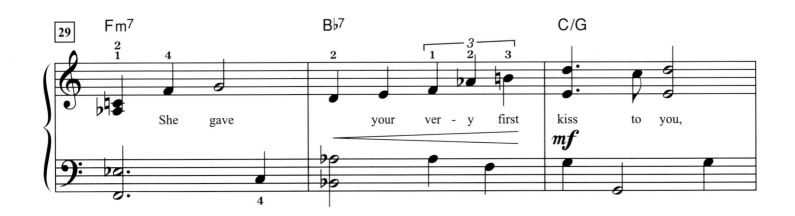

She gave your ver - y first kiss to you, *mf*

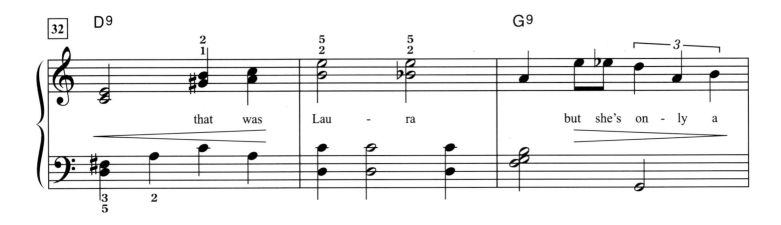

that was Lau - ra but she's on - ly a

1.
dream.

2.
dream. *rit. e dim.* *p*

This classic song was featured in the 1955 movie *Love Is a Many Splendored Thing*. The movie went on to win an Academy Award for Best Song. The best-selling version of the song was recorded by The Four Aces which reached #1 on the Billboard charts in 1955. "Love Is a Many Splendored Thing" has been recorded by Frank Sinatra and Andy Williams, and in 2006 Barry Manilow included the hit on his album *The Greatest Songs of the Fifties*.

LOVE IS A MANY SPLENDORED THING
Love Is a Many Splendered Thing

Music by Sammy Fain
Lyric by Paul Francis Webster

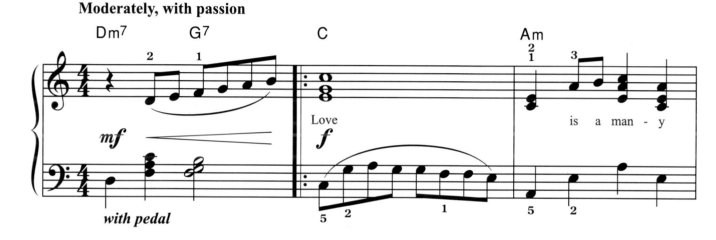

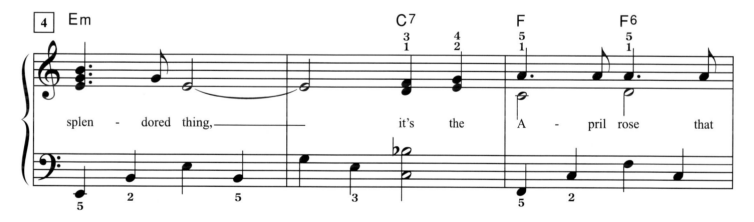

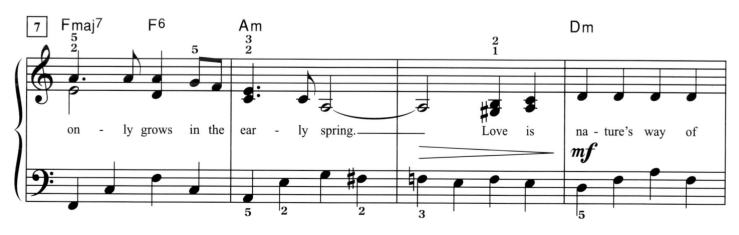

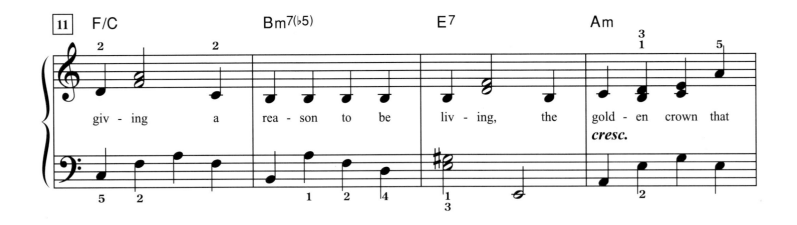

11 F/C ... Bm7(♭5) ... E7 ... Am

giv - ing a rea - son to be liv - ing, the gold - en crown that
cresc.

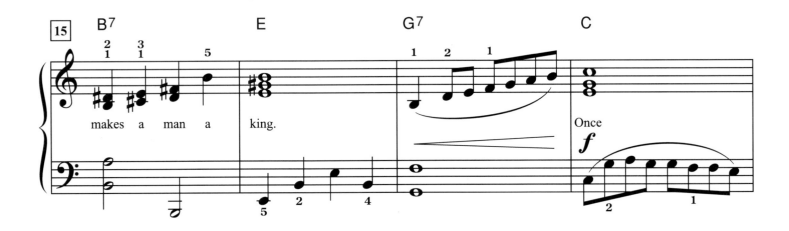

15 B7 ... E ... G7 ... C

makes a man a king.

Once
f

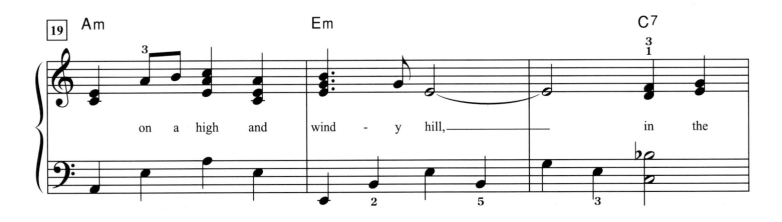

19 Am ... Em ... C7

on a high and wind - y hill,_____ in the

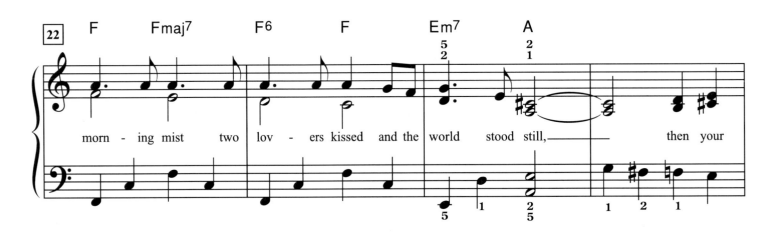

22 F Fmaj7 ... F6 ... F ... Em7 ... A

morn - ing mist two lov - ers kissed and the world stood still,_____ then your

The 1983 film *Risky Business* catapulted a young Tom Cruise to movie stardom and cemented the Bob Seeger hit "Old Time Rock and Roll." In the movie, Cruise dances around the house to this song to celebrate his freedom while his parents are out of town.

OLD TIME ROCK AND ROLL

Risky Business

Words and Music by
George Jackson and Thomas E. Jones III

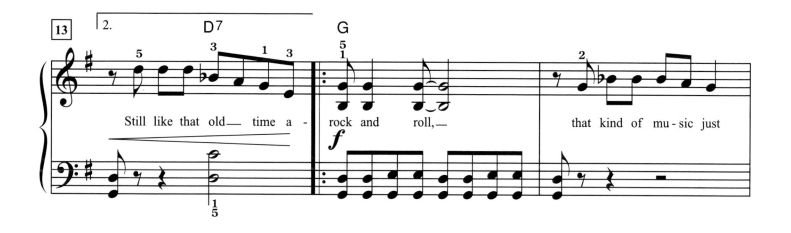

13 | 2. — D7 — | G
Still like that old— time a - | rock and roll,— | that kind of mu - sic just

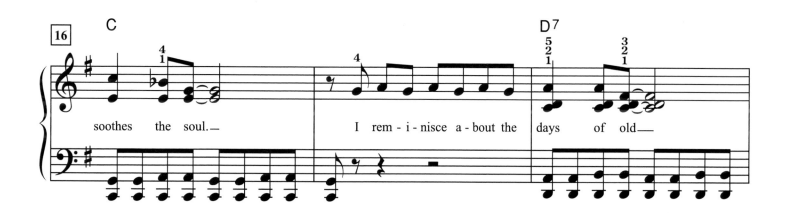

16 | C | | D7
soothes the soul.— | I rem - i - nisce a - bout the | days of old—

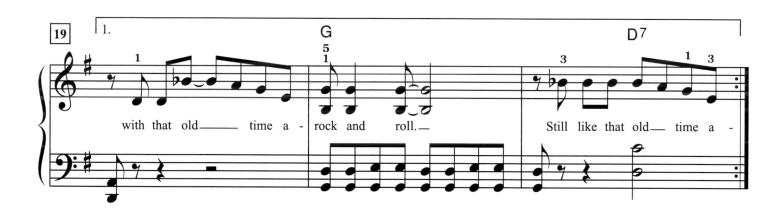

19 | 1. — G | D7
with that old——— time a - | rock and roll.— | Still like that old— time a -

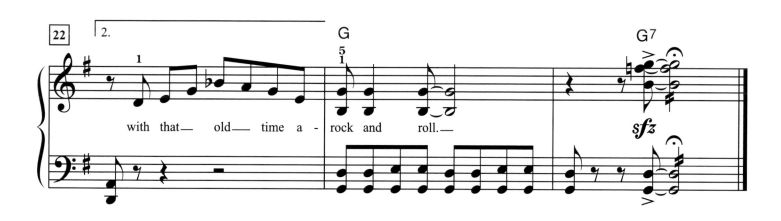

22 | 2. — G | G7
with that— old— time a - | rock and roll.— |
sfz

"Over the Rainbow" was featured in MGM's classic 1939 film *The Wizard of Oz*. It was famously sung in the film by Judy Garland who played Dorothy, a Kansas farm girl who yearns for a better life. "Over the Rainbow" has been voted the #1 movie song by the American Film Institute. In addition to being the signature song for Garland, it has also been the signature song for two great singers whose lives and careers ended prematurely—Eva Cassidy and Israel "Iz" Kamakawiwoʻole.

OVER THE RAINBOW
The Wizard of Oz

Music by Harold Arlen
Lyrics by E.Y. Harburg

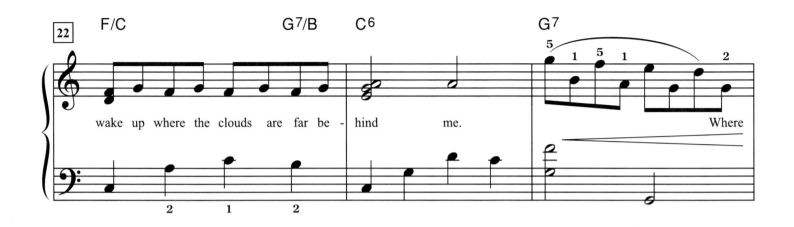

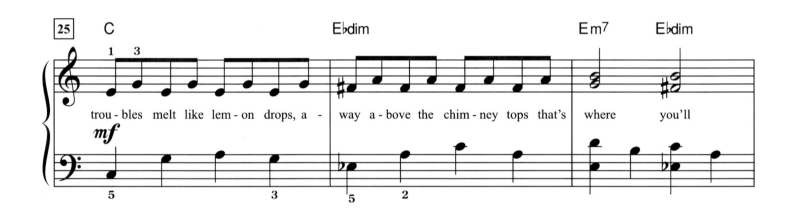

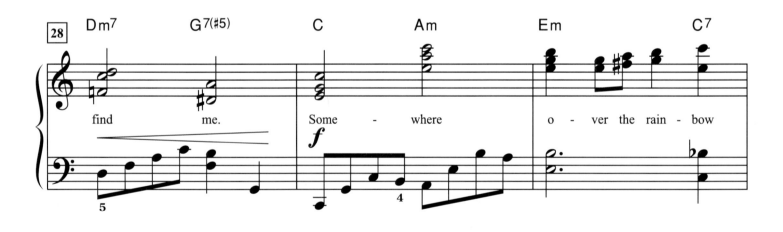

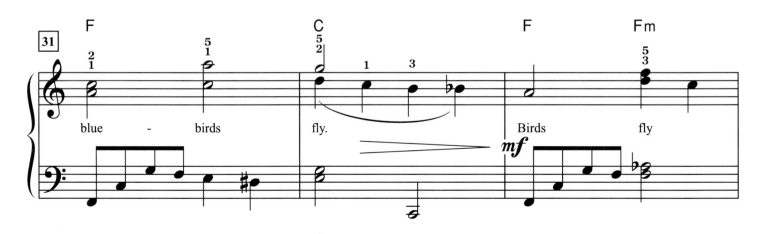

The Little Mermaid is an 1837 fairy tale by Hans Christian Andersen. In 1989, Walt Disney Pictures released an animated version of *The Little Mermaid* featuring an award-winning score by Alan Menken and Howard Ashman. "Part of Your World" is sung by Ariel, a mermaid, who longs to be a part of the human world.

PART OF YOUR WORLD
Walt Disney's *The Little Mermaid*

Music by Alan Menken
Lyrics by Howard Ashman

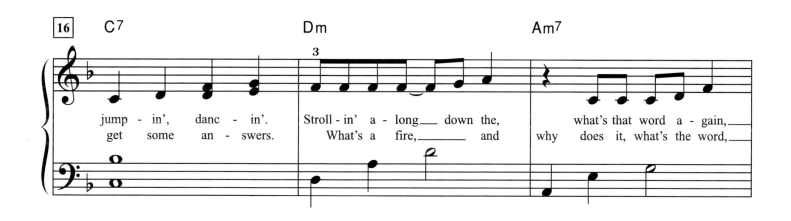

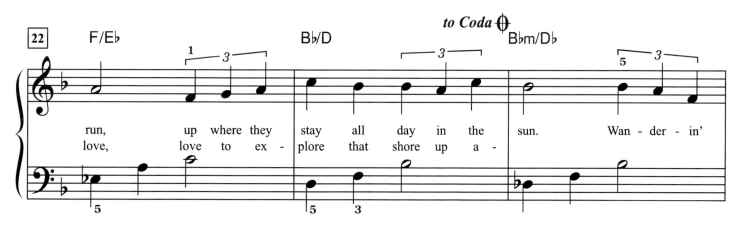

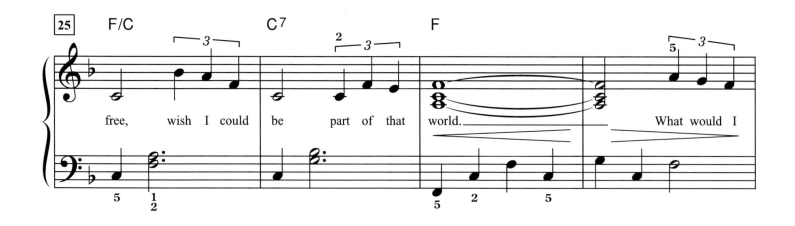

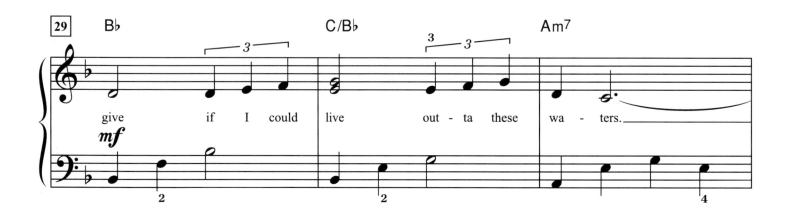

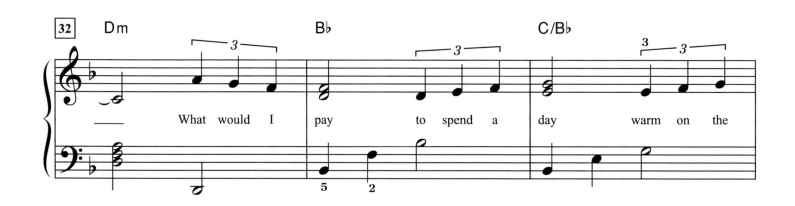

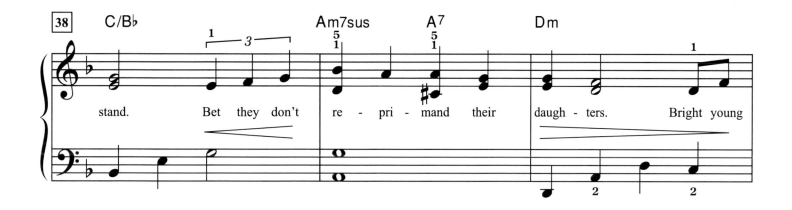

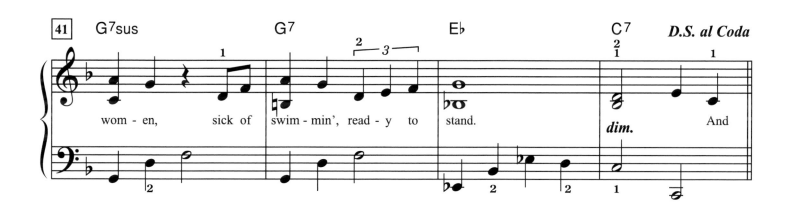

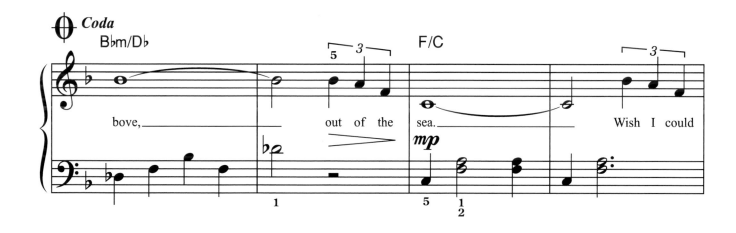

The Pink Panther is a series of comedic films spanning the years 1963–2006. The main character is bumbling French detective, Jacques Clouseau (famously played by Peter Sellars in the earlier films), who manages to survive countless brushes with death despite his clumsiness and aloof demeanor. The jazzy theme is famous for its chromatically moving parallel fifths and stealth character.

THE PINK PANTHER
The Pink Panther

By Henry Mancini

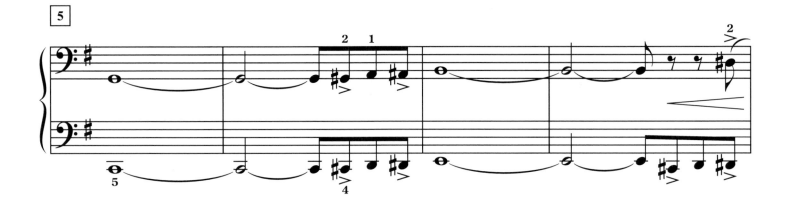

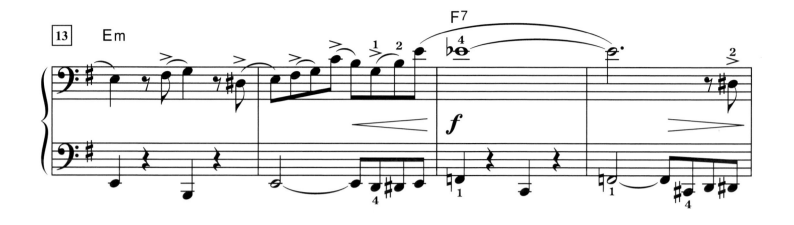

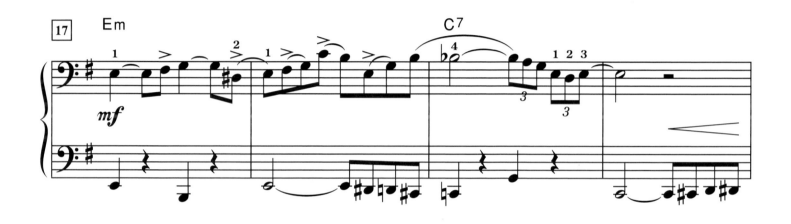

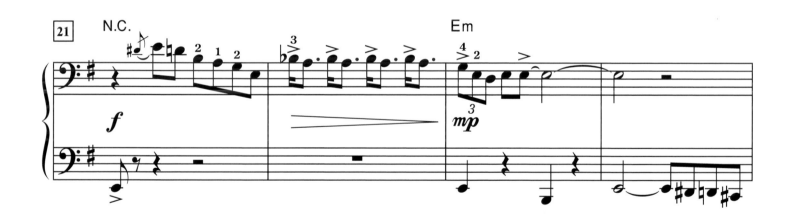

B. J. Thomas recorded "Raindrops Keep Fallin' on My Head" in 1969 for the movie *Butch Cassidy and the Sundance Kid*. It accompanies a dialogue-less scene in the film where Butch pursues Etta Place, Sundance's girlfriend. The song won the Academy Award in 1969 for Best Original Song and became a worldwide hit.

Raindrops Keep Fallin' on My Head

Butch Cassidy and the Sundance Kid

Words by Hal David
Music by Burt Bacharach

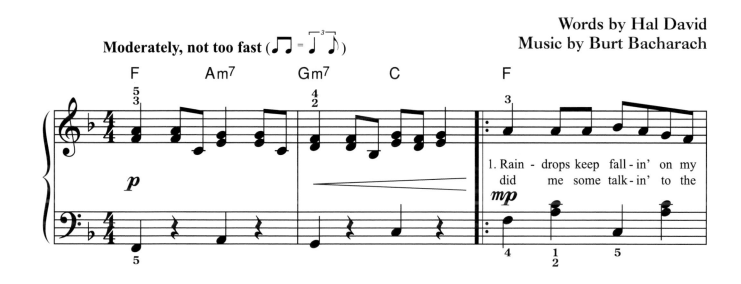

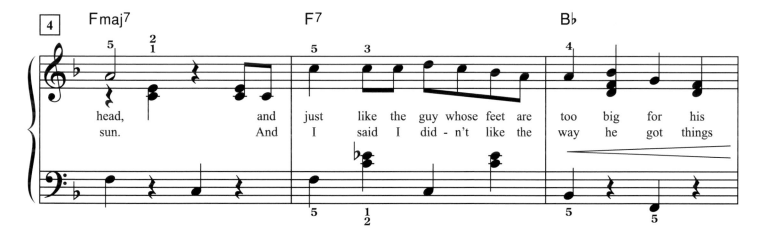

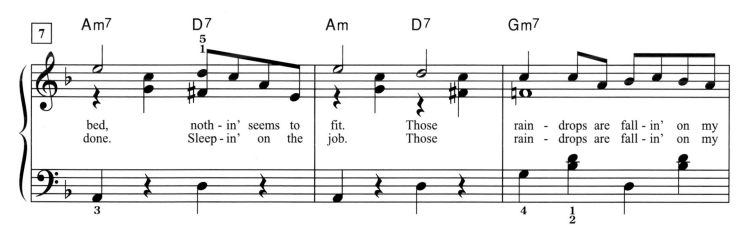

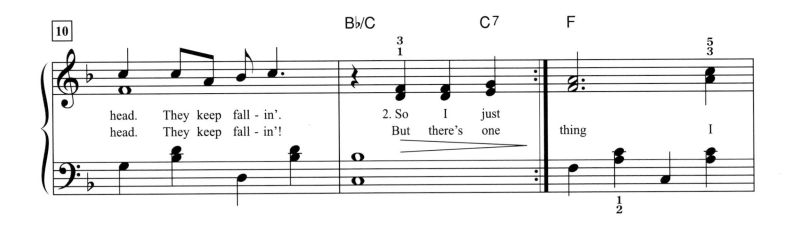

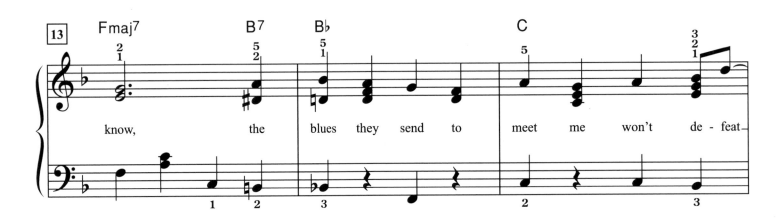

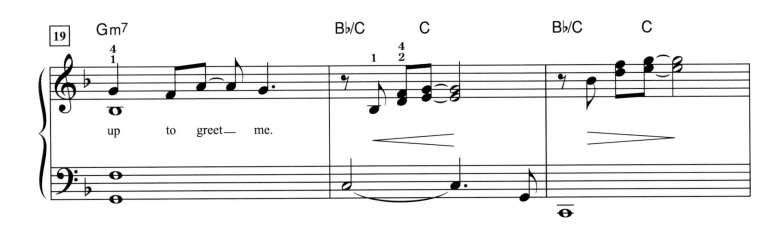

Raindrops keep fallin' on my head, but that doesn't mean my eyes will

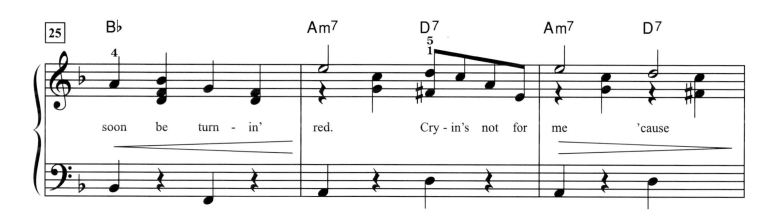

soon be turnin' red. Cryin's not for me 'cause

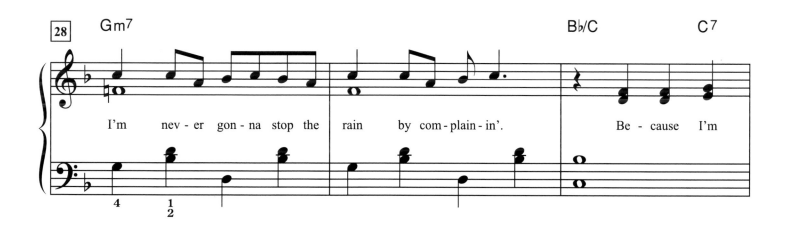

I'm never gonna stop the rain by complainin'. Because I'm

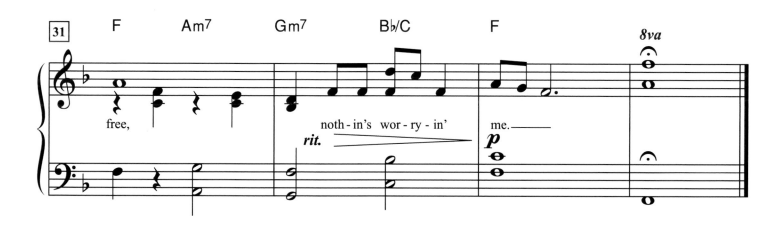

free, nothin's worryin' me.

John Williams initially composed "Raiders March" for the 1981 film *Raiders of the Lost Ark,* starring Harrison Ford and directed by Steven Spielberg. The Oscar-nominated score has since been used in all four installments of the *Indiana Jones* franchise. "Raiders March" was recorded by the London Symphony Orchestra.

RAIDERS MARCH
Raiders of the Lost Ark

Music by JOHN WILLIAMS

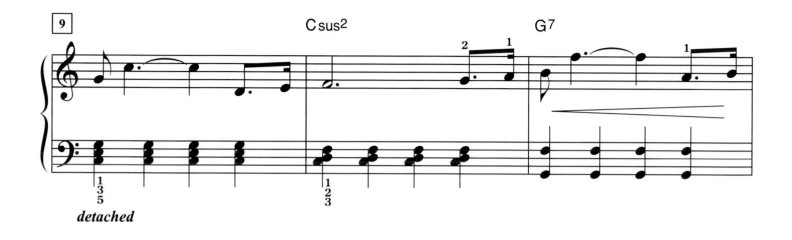

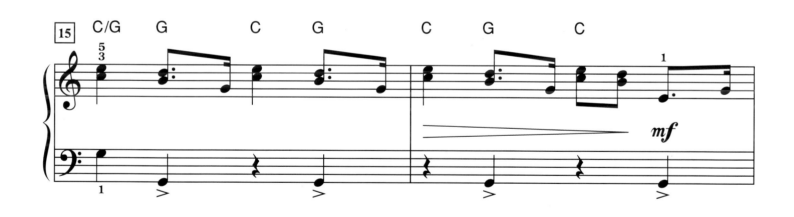

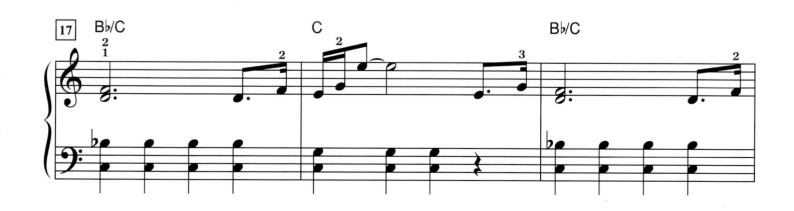

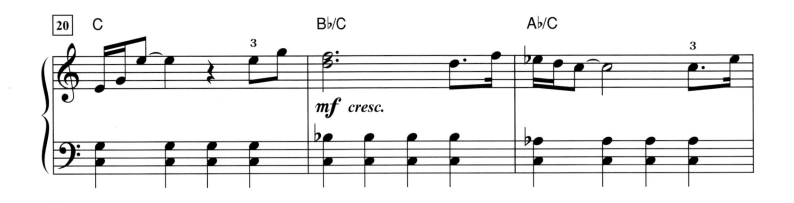

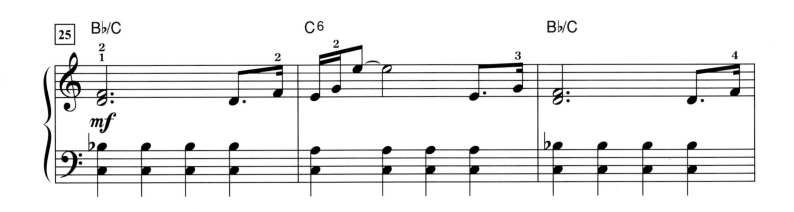

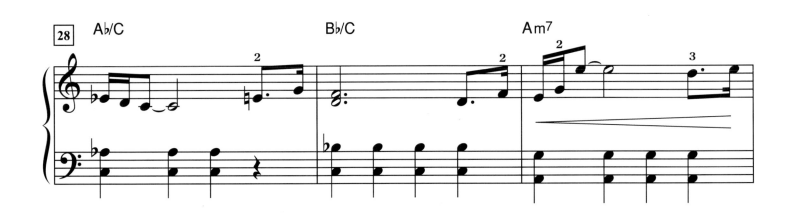

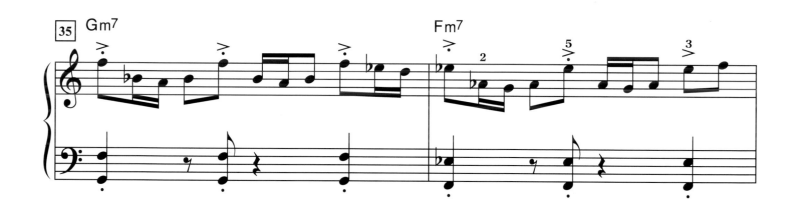

Kenny Ascher and Paul Williams received an Oscar nomination for this song, which originally appeared in *The Muppet Movie* in 1979. Jim Henson, the voice of Kermit the Frog, sang the song with a wistfulness that turned it into an unlikely hit. It may be the only time a frog made it to the Billboard charts!

THE RAINBOW CONNECTION

The Muppet Movie

Words and Music by
Paul Williams and Kenneth L. Ascher

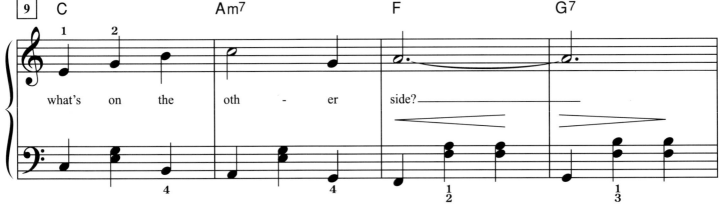

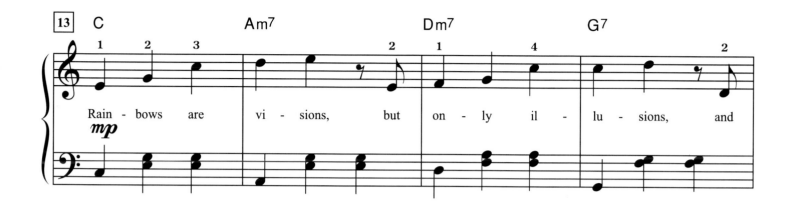

13 | C   Am7   Dm7   G7

Rain - bows are vi - sions, but on - ly il - lu - sions, and

mp

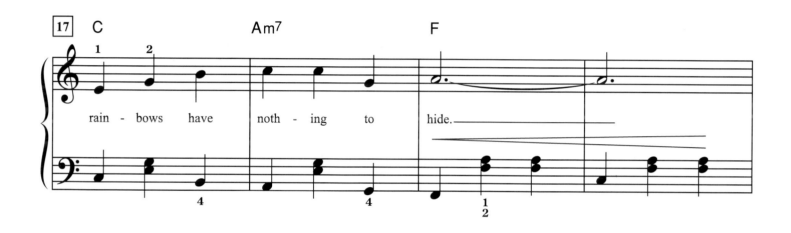

17 | C   Am7   F

rain - bows have noth - ing to hide.

21 | Fmaj7

So we've been told, and some choose to be - lieve it.

mf

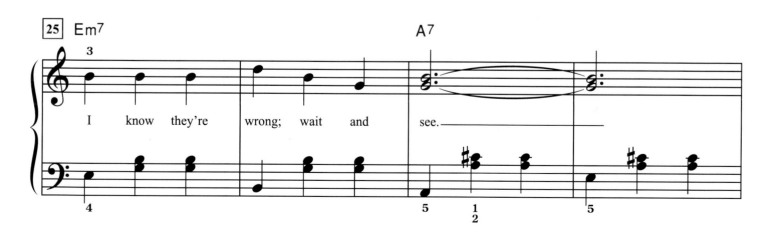

25 | Em7   A7

I know they're wrong; wait and see.

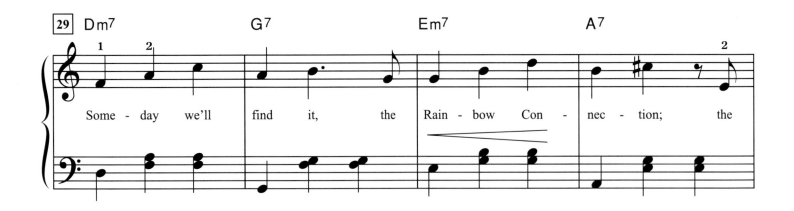

Some - day we'll find it, the Rain - bow Con - nec - tion; the

to Coda 1.

lov - ers, the dream - ers,——— and me.

mp

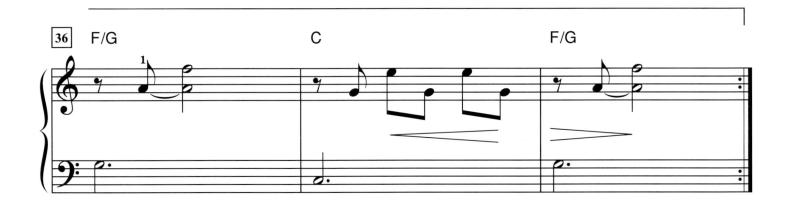

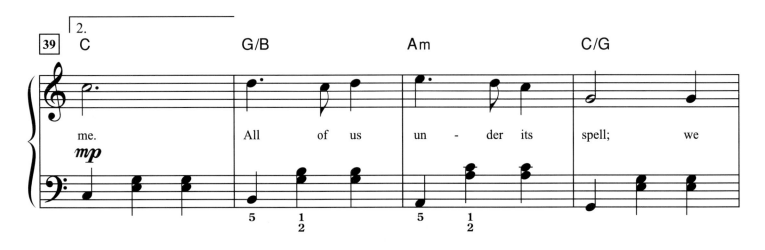

2.

me. All of us un - der its spell; we

mp

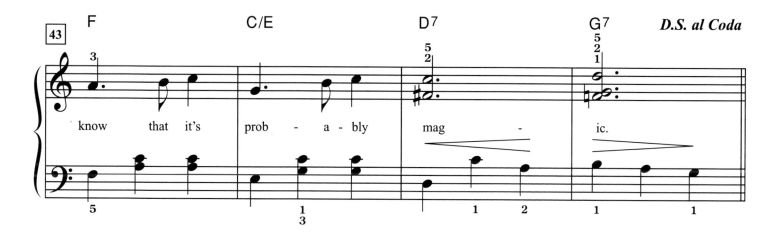

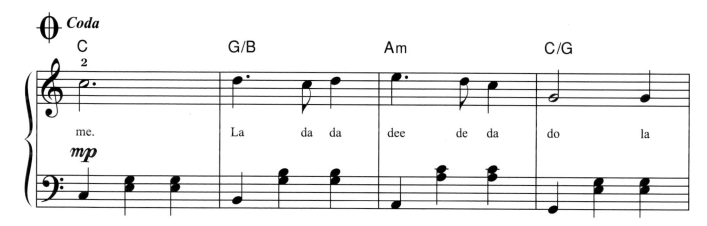

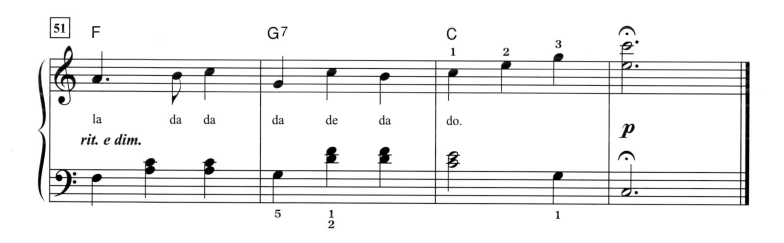

Verse 2:
Who said that every wish would be heard and answered
When wished on the morning star?
Somebody thought of that, and someone believed it;
Look what it's done so far.
What's so amazing that keeps us stargazing,
And what do we think we might see?
Someday we'll find it, the Rainbow Connection;
The lovers, the dreamers, and me.

Verse 3:
Have you been half asleep and have you heard voices?
I've heard them calling my name.
Is this the sweet sound that calls the young sailors?
The voice might be one and the same.
I've heard it too many times to ignore it.
It's something that I'm s'posed to be.
Someday we'll find it, the Rainbow Connection;
The lovers, the dreamers, and me.

"(We're Gonna) Rock Around the Clock" is considered the first rock and roll song, and was recorded by Bill Haley & His Comets in 1954. However, it did not hit the pop charts until it played during the opening credits of the 1955 film *Blackboard Jungle*. Following its film "debut," it topped the American Billboard charts for eight weeks.

(We're Gonna) Rock Around the Clock

Blackboard Jungle

Words and Music by
Max C. Freedman and Jimmy De Knight

The 1979 film *The Rose* is loosely based on the rise and fall of rock star Janis Joplin. Great performances were contributed by Bette Midler as the rock star and Alan Bates as her manager. The film includes this popular song, written by Amanda McBroom, featuring beautiful, timeless lyrics.

THE ROSE
The Rose

Words and Music by
Amanda McBroom

The image of Gene Kelly singing the title song from 1952's *Singin' in the Rain* is one of the most iconic film images of all time. Interestingly, the script initially called for the song to be sung by Kelly and his co-stars, Debbie Reynolds and Donald O'Connor. It was later changed to a solo dance routine, with Kelly splashing and twirling around in the rain.

SINGIN' IN THE RAIN

Singin' in the Rain

Music by Nacio Herb Brown
Lyric by Arthur Freed

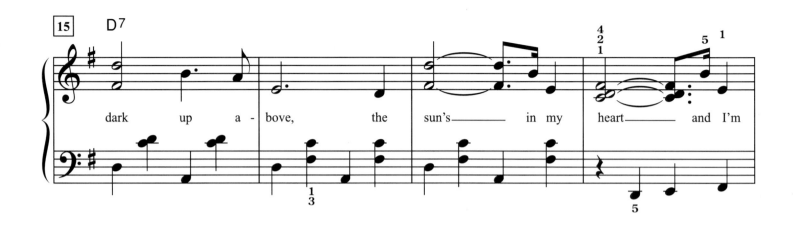

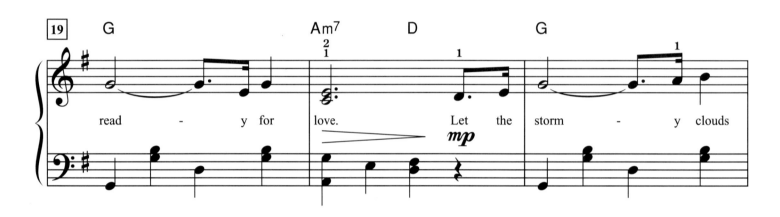

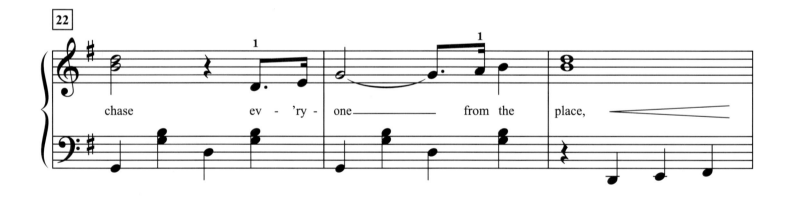

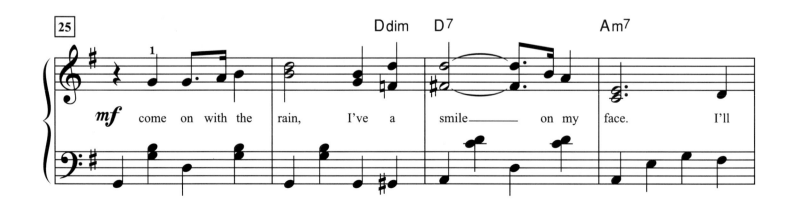

walk   down   the   lane   with a   hap - py re - frain,   and

sing - in', ____   just   sing - in' in ____ the   rain.

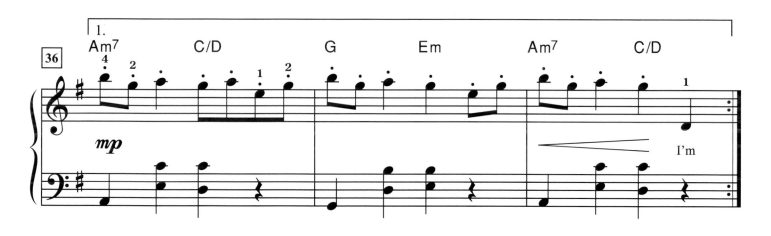

I'm

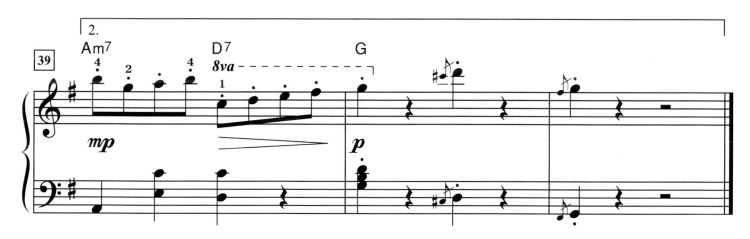

Doctor Zhivago (published in 1957) is an epic novel set against the backdrop of the 1917 Russian Revolution. In 1965, it was made into an award-winning film, directed by David Lean, starring Omar Sharif (Yuri Zhivago) and Julie Christie (Larissa "Lara" Antipova). Maurice Jarre composed the music for the film which became popular worldwide. The music that accompanied Lara's scenes, "Lara's Theme," was particularly well-received, and in 1966 Ray Conniff added lyrics to the music and recorded it with his Ray Conniff Singers, entitling it "Somewhere My Love."

SOMEWHERE MY LOVE
Doctor Zhivago

Music by Maurice Jarre
Lyrics by Paul Francis Webster

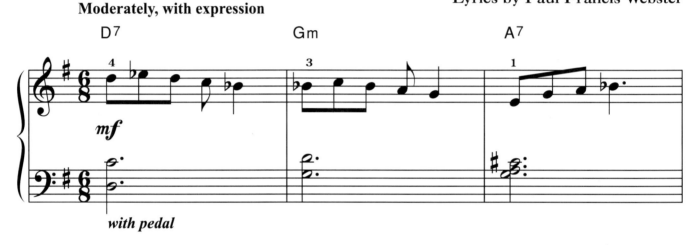

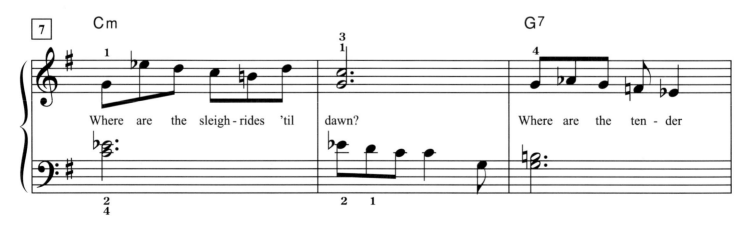

On May 25, 1977 George Lucas introduced the world to *Star Wars,* one of the most successful, popular and influential films of all time, a science fiction masterpiece. The movie's dazzling special effects not only won over an ongoing fan base but also directed the film industry's focus to big-budget blockbuster productions. The film's soundtrack—performed by the London Symphony Orchestra with John Williams conducting—was voted #1 by the American Film Institute in 2005.

STAR WARS® (MAIN TITLE)

Star Wars

Music by JOHN WILLIAMS

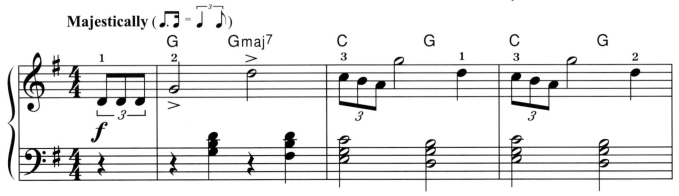

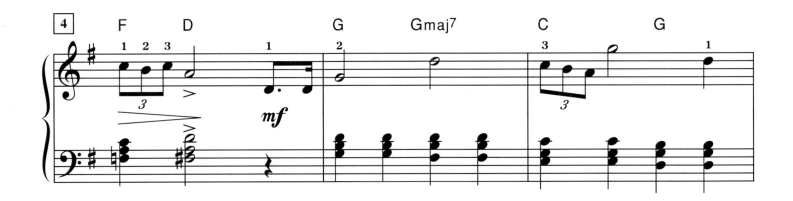

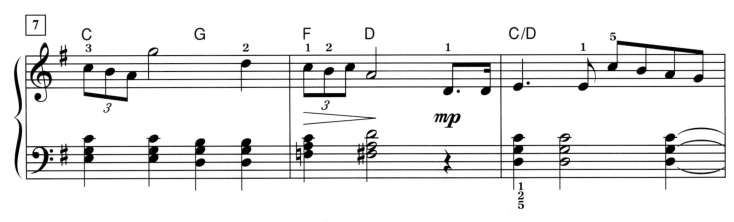

Disco originated in the United States in the early '70s, derived from funk and soul music, and the term "disco" originated from the French word "discothèque" meaning nightclub. A number of musicians were well known for this up-tempo dance music: ABBA, Barry White, Donna Summer, Gloria Gaynor, KC and The Sunshine Band, and the Village People, to name a few. The 1977 film *Saturday Night Fever* helped established disco as a genre. The Bee Gees' "Stayin' Alive" was the first track on the soundtrack for the film and provided the music for the opening scene.

STAYIN' ALIVE

Saturday Night Fever

Words and Music by Barry Gibb,
Maurice Gibb and Robin Gibb

Bruce Springsteen wrote "Streets of Philadelphia" at the request of *Philadelphia* director Johnathan Demme. It garnered an Academy Award and Grammy for Springsteen as well as success on the pop charts in the U. S. and abroad. Tom Hanks, who played the lead role, won an Academy Award for Best Actor.

STREETS OF PHILADELPHIA

Philadelphia

Words and Music by
Bruce Springsteen

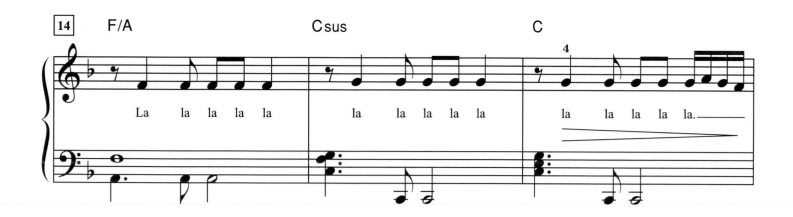

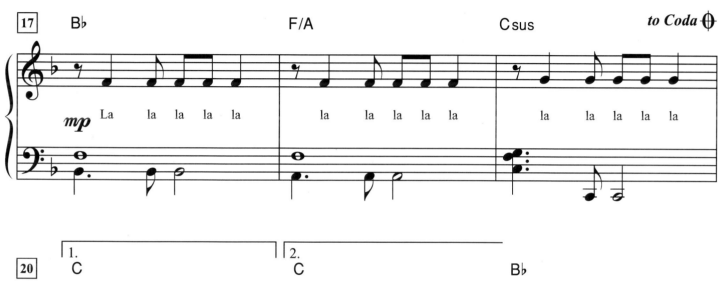

Verse 2:
I walked the avenue 'til my legs felt like stone.
I heard the voices of friends vanished and gone.
At night I could hear the blood in my veins
Just as black and whispering as the rain
On the streets of Philadelphia.

Verse 3:
The night has fallen, I'm lyin' awake.
I can feel myself fading away.
So, receive me, brother, with your faithless kiss,
Or will we leave each other alone like this
On the streets of Philadelphia?

"A Whole New World" is the hit single from Walt Disney's animated feature *Aladdin* (1992). In the film it was sung by Brad (Caleb) Kane and Lea Salonga (the singing voices for Aladdin and Princess Jasmine) and during the closing credits by Peabo Bryson and Regina Belle. The ballad won the Academy Award for Best Original Song.

A WHOLE NEW WORLD
Walt Disney's *Aladdin*

Words by Tim Rice
Music by Alan Menken

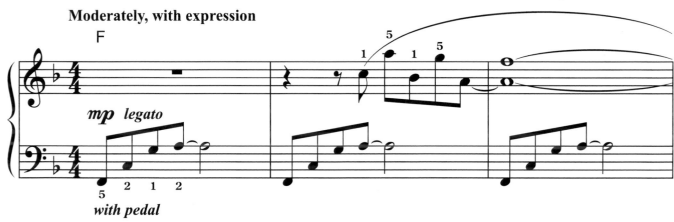

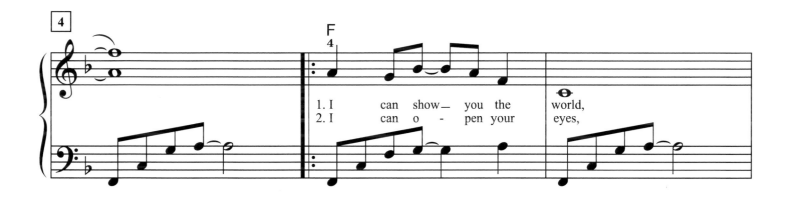

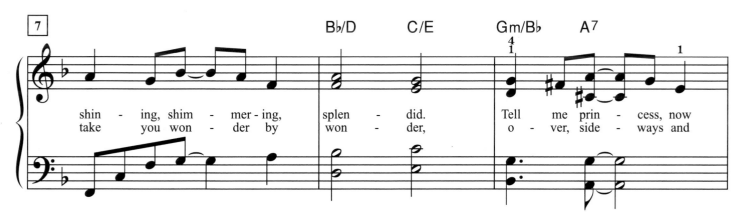

The new wave band Berlin formed in Orange County, California, in the late '70s. Their first single "The Metro" is a prime example of the new wave genre—blending punk, pop, and cutting-edge synthesizer technology. The band recorded the love song "Take My Breath Away" for *Top Gun*, the 1986 fighter pilot film starring Tom Cruise, Kelly McGillis, and Val Kilmer. The song reached #1 on the Billboard Hot 100 and won an Academy Award and a Golden Globe Award for Best Original Song.

TAKE MY BREATH AWAY

Top Gun

Music by Giorgio Moroder
Words by Tom Whitlock

"Under the Sea," from 1989's *The Little Mermaid,* won the Academy Award for Best Song. Sung by Sebastian, a crab, the calypso-styled piece is meant to sway Ariel to see the good of living in the sea. "Part of Your World," the other huge hit from the movie, is on page 88.

Under the Sea
Walt Disney's *The Little Mermaid*

Lyrics by Howard Ashman
Music by Alan Menken

Oscar-, Grammy-, and Emmy-winning Michel Legrand wrote "The Windmills of Your Mind" for the 1968 film *The Thomas Crown Affair*, starring Steve McQueen and Faye Dunaway. The movie is modeled after the life of a Belgian art thief. It received the Academy Award that year for Best Original Song.

THE WINDMILLS OF YOUR MIND
The Thomas Crown Affair

Words by Alan and Marilyn Bergman
Music by Michel Legrand

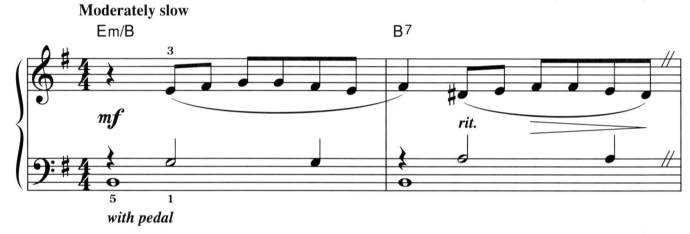

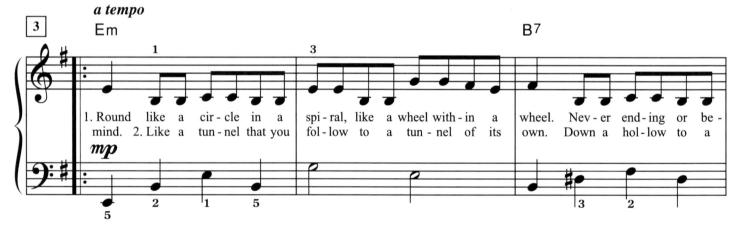

1. Round like a cir - cle in a spi - ral, like a wheel with - in a wheel. Nev - er end - ing or be -
2. Like a tun - nel that you fol - low to a tun - nel of its own. Down a hol - low to a

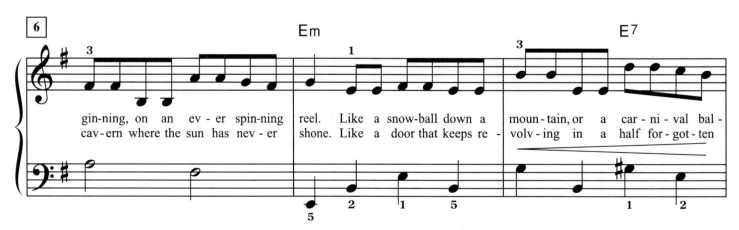

gin - ning, on an ev - er spin - ning reel. Like a snow - ball down a moun - tain, or a car - ni - val bal -
cav - ern where the sun has nev - er shone. Like a door that keeps re - volv - ing in a half for - got - ten

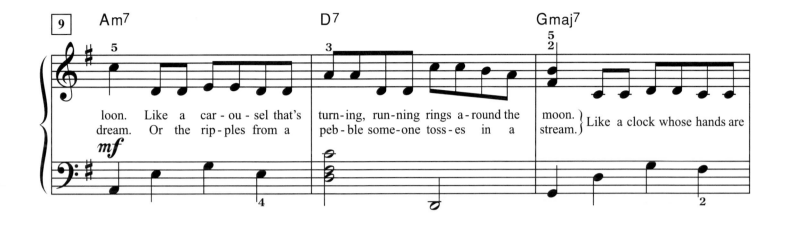

9 | Am7 | D7 | Gmaj7

loon. Like a car-ou-sel that's / turn-ing, run-ning rings a-round the / moon. } Like a clock whose hands are

dream. Or the rip-ples from a / peb-ble some-one toss-es in a / stream. } Like a clock whose hands are

mf

12 | Cmaj7 | F#m7(♭5) | B7

sweep-ing past the min-utes of its / face. And the world is like an / ap-ple whirl-ing si-lent-ly in

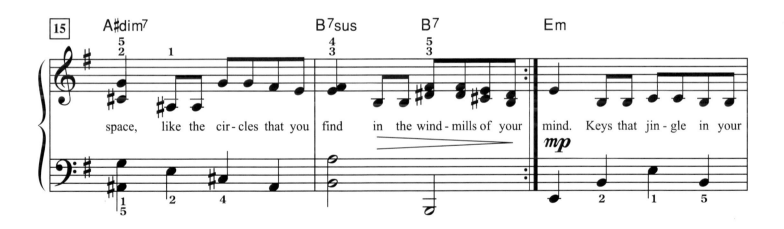

15 | A#dim7 | B7sus | B7 | Em

space, like the cir-cles that you / find in the wind-mills of your / mind. Keys that jin-gle in your

mp

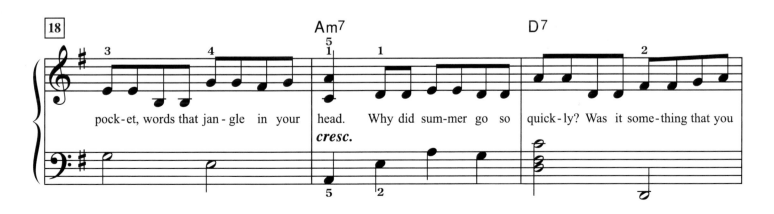

18 | Am7 | D7

pock-et, words that jan-gle in your / head. Why did sum-mer go so / quick-ly? Was it some-thing that you

cresc.

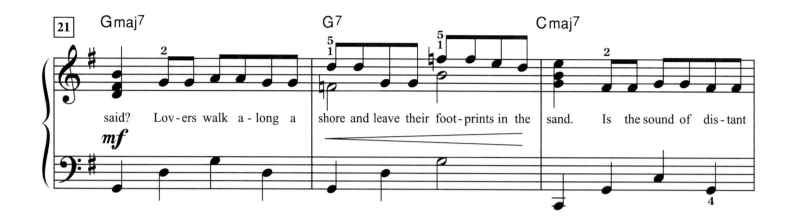

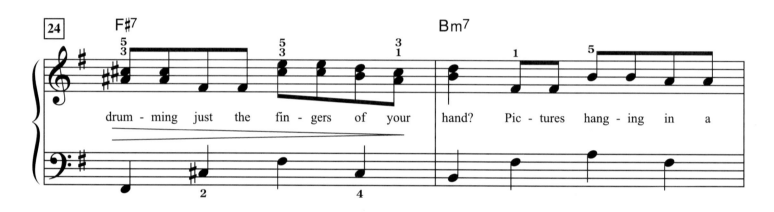

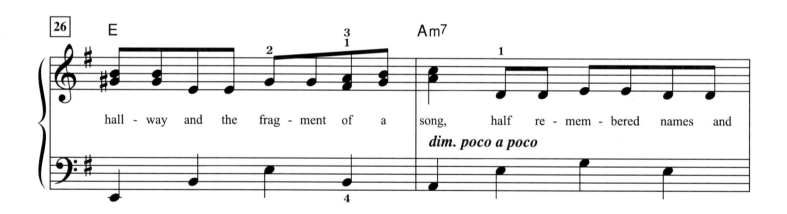

"Wind Beneath My Wings" is known as Bette Midler's signature song. She recorded it in 1989 for the dramatic film *Beaches,* a movie in which she also starred. The single was a #1 hit and also won Record of the Year and Song of the Year at the 1990 Grammy Awards. A number of artists (Sheena Easton, Roger Whittaker, Gary Morris, Gladys Knight, and Lou Rawls) had recorded the song before Midler, yet none were as successful.

THE WIND BENEATH MY WINGS
Beaches

Words and Music by
Larry Henley and Jeff Silbar

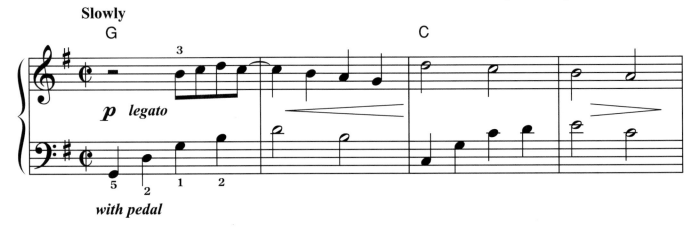

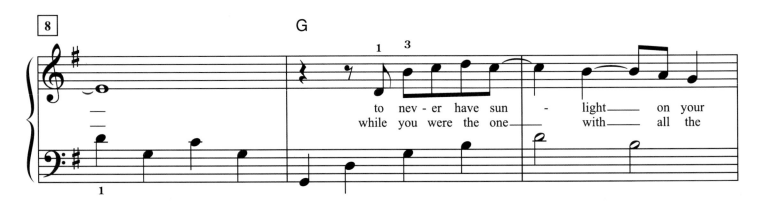